CHINA AND THE THIRD WORLD

CHINA AND THE THIRD WORLD

Champion or
Challenger?

Edited by

Lillian Craig Harris
United States Department of State

Robert L. Worden
Library of Congress

 *Auburn House Publishing Company*
Dover, Massachusetts

Library of Congress Cataloging in Publication Data

Main entry under title:

China and the Third World.

    Includes bibliographies and index.
    1. Developing countries—Foreign relations—China—
Addresses, essays, lectures. 2. China—Foreign relations
—Developing countries—Addresses, essays, lectures.
I. Harris, Lillian Craig. II. Worden, Robert L.
D888.C6C48   1986   327.510172′4   85-30690
ISBN 0-86569-142-8

Printed in the United States of America

To Joseph S. Sebes, S.J.
Teacher, inspiration, and friend.

PREFACE

The purpose of this book, as conceived amidst the intellectual milieu of a bygone Association for Asian Studies annual meeting, was to present a thematic approach to China's evolving role in the Third World. Rather than address various Third World regions in separate chapters, we chose to analyze the China–Third World question from a variety of perspectives, each of which would exemplify the general Chinese Third World policy and its specific application to the developing world in a particular subject area. Recognizing our own limitations in such a large-scale project, we approached several scholars who had previously given thought to these particular subject areas, although not necessarily with regard to the China–Third World perspective. The result is this volume of seven original chapters, written independently, and, in some cases, with divergent conclusions. As editors of this volume, we want to thank the individual contributors for their willingness to write their chapters and undergo the trials of redrafting their already well-crafted ideas into the format we envisioned.

As editors of this book and observers of China, we are aware of the American propensity to adopt a superior attitude toward China, one which either consciously or unconsciously assumes that "we understand the Chinese" and are ourselves free from the international and domestic errors they have made as well as from the political, diplomatic, and rhetorical devices they employ. It is not our intention in any way to call the Chinese to task for their present advocacy of an independent foreign policy with its strong Third World ingredient or to criticize them for exhibiting the self-interest that all nations must use as the starting point of any policy. Despite what may appear to some as harshness in portions of the analysis in this volume, our attempt is not to criticize but rather to strive for a clearer understanding of the difficulties faced by developing China as it seeks to create for itself a position of international security and domestic equilibrium. We have, in fact, considerable admiration for the successes China has achieved during recent years at home and abroad and anticipate that a strong and stable China will continue to evolve toward an ever more significant position of world leadership as at least a nominal member of the Third World and, in many ways, as a model for Third World approaches to international and domestic problems.

We wish to express our gratitude to Dr. Wang Chi, Head of the Chinese and Korean Section of the Library of Congress, for providing the beautiful calligraphy for the book's Chinese title. We also are grateful to our professional colleagues who have shared their views with us on China's foreign policies and rendered useful criticisms of our efforts. We are appreciative of the International Studies Association, which afforded the contributors the opportunity to present their ideas on China's Third World policies at the 26th Annual Convention in Washington, D.C. in 1985. We also thank the Center for Strategic and International Studies, Georgetown University, which has graciously given permission to use material from its *Washington Papers, China's Foreign Policy Toward the Third World,* by Lillian Craig Harris, quoted in Chapter 1. The editors of the *Far Eastern Economic Review* have been similarly generous in allowing us to use data from their journal cited in Chapter 6. To the staff of Auburn House Publishing Company, we owe our thanks for helping this volume become a reality. Not least of all, we want to express our loving appreciation to our respective spouses, Alan and Norma, for their bemused patience in observing this undertaking.

Finally, several of the authors are current or former employees of the U.S. Government; they wish to emphasize that the conclusions drawn in their chapters do not necessarily represent the views of their respective agencies.

CONTENTS

TABULAR MATERIAL

ABBREVIATIONS

ADB	Asian Development Bank
ANC	African National Congress
ASEAN	Association of Southeast Asian Nations
Banyue Tan	Semimonthly Talks (Beijing)
BCP	Burma Communist Party
CANA	Caribbean News Agency
CCP	Chinese Communist Party
CIA	Central Intelligence Agency
cif	cost, insurance, and freight
CPP	Communist Party of the Philippines
ESCAP	Economic and Social Council for Asia and the Pacific (UN)
FAO	Food and Agricultural Organization (UN)
FBIS	Foreign Broadcast Information Service (U.S.)
fob	free on board
FMLN	Farabundo Marti National Liberation Front
FNLA	National Front for the Liberation of Angola
GATT	General Agreement on Tariffs and Trade
GNP	gross national product
Guoji Wenti Yanjiu	Journal of International Studies (Beijing)
Hongqi	Red Flag (Beijing)
IAEA	International Atomic Energy Agency (UN)
IDA	International Development Association
IMF	International Monetary Fund

IOC	International Olympic Committee
JANA	Jamahiriya News Agency
Jiefangjun Bao	Liberation Army Daily (Beijing)
Liaowang	Outlook (Beijing)
MPLA	Popular Movement for the Liberation of Angola
NATO	North Atlantic Treaty Organization
NPA	New People's Army
OAU	Organization of African Unity
OPANAL	Organization for the Prohibition of Nuclear Weapons in Latin America
OPEC	Organization of Petroleum Exporting Countries
PAC	Pan-Africanist Congress
PDPA	People's Democratic Party of Afghanistan
PKI	Indonesian Communist Party
PLO	Palestine Liberation Organization
PRC	People's Republic of China
Renmin Ribao	People's Daily (Beijing)
SEATO	Southeast Asia Treaty Organization
Shijie Jingji	World Economics (Beijing)
Shijie Zhishi	World Knowledge (Beijing)
SRV	Socialist Republic of Vietnam
SWAPO	South-West Africa People's Organization
TanZam Railway	Tanzania-Zambia Railway (Also known as TANZAR)
UIO	Union of International Organizations
UNCTAD	United Nations Conference on Trade and Development
UNDP	United Nations Development Programme
UNESCO	United Nations Educational, Social and Cultural Organization
UNIDO	United Nations Industrial Development Organization
UNITA	National Union for the Total Independence of Angola
Xinhua	New China News Agency
ZANU	Zimbabwe African National Union
Zhongguo Xinwen She	China News Service

THE EDITORS AND CONTRIBUTORS

Lillian Craig Harris, the daughter and granddaughter of missionaries to China, holds a B.A. in Biblical Education from Columbia Bible College, an M.A. in journalism from Syracuse University, an M.A. in Modern Middle East History from the American University of Beirut, and a Ph.D. in Modern Asian History from Georgetown University. For several years she has been a political analyst in the U.S. Department of State's Bureau of Intelligence and Research and is also a member of the Executive Committee of the Liberal Studies Program at Georgetown University, where she teaches courses on China. Dr. Harris is the author of numerous articles on China and of *China's Foreign Policy Toward the Third World* (Washington, D.C.: Center for Strategic and International Studies, Georgetown University, 1985). Westview Press will publish her survey of Libya in 1986.

Robert L. Worden has been a China specialist at Library of Congress's Federal Research Division since 1973 and currently is head of the division's Asia Section. He received his B.A. from St. Bonaventure University, St. Bonaventure, N.Y., and an M.A. and Ph.D. in Asian history from Georgetown University. He has authored several journal articles on Chinese foreign policy and history and contributed chapters to *Dimensions of China's Foreign Relations* (Chun-tu Hsueh, editor, New York: Praeger Publishers, 1977); *China's Foreign Relations: Selected Studies* (F. Gilbert Chan and Ka-che Yip, editors, Baltimore: School of Law, University of Maryland, 1980); and *China's Foreign Relations: New Perspectives* (Chun-tu Hsueh, editor, New York: Praeger Publishers, 1982). He has taught Asian history courses at Georgetown University and has been a guest lecturer at the University of Maryland, The American University, The Johns Hopkins University, and the Department of State's Foreign Service Institute.

Carol Lee Hamrin is a Research Specialist for China at the U.S. Department of State, and Professorial Lecturer at the School of Advanced International Studies, The Johns Hopkins University, Washington, D.C. She received her B.A. from St. Olaf College, Northfield, Minnesota, and her Ph.D. from the University of Wisconsin. Dr. Hamrin is co-editor with Timothy Cheek of *China's Establishment Intellectuals* (M.E. Sharpe, Inc., 1985) and with Merle Goldman and Timothy Cheek of *Chinese Intellectuals and the State: Search for a New Relationship* (forthcoming).

Bruce D. Larkin is Professor of Politics and Fellow of Cowell College, University of California at Santa Cruz, where he was a founding member of the faculty. He received his B.A. from the University of Chicago in 1954 and a Ph.D. from Harvard University in 1966. He has taught as a Fulbright Lecturer at Keio University and Tsukuba University in Tokyo, and from 1975 to 1977 was Director of the University of California Study Center at the Chinese University of Hong Kong. A specialist on international politics and contemporary Chinese foreign policy, Professor Larkin is the author of *China and Africa, 1949–1970: The Foreign Policy of the People's Republic of China* (Berkeley: University of California Press, 1971). He is currently engaged on a manuscript on the theory of war.

Robert A. Manning is a foreign affairs analyst with *U.S. News and World Report* in Washington, D.C. Since 1979 he has written extensively on Asia, including a stint as Washington correspondent of the *Far Eastern Economic Review*. His articles also have appeared in *Foreign Affairs, Foreign Policy, New Republic*, and other journals. Mr. Manning received his B.A. in history from California State University, Northridge. He has traveled extensively in Asia.

Sarah-Ann Smith is a free-lance consultant and writer. She formerly served as a Foreign Service Officer with the U.S. Department of State for 12 years, 10 of which were spent in China-related assignments. She holds a B.A. from Queens College, Charlotte, North Carolina, and a Ph.D. in international studies from The American University, Washington, D.C. Her dissertation consisted of an analysis of the conceptual bases of Chinese foreign policy.

Robert G. Sutter has been a specialist in Asian affairs with the Congressional Research Service of the Library of Congress since

1977. Previously, he served for eight years as an analyst of Chinese foreign policy with the Central Intelligence Agency. Since 1980 he has also held special assignments dealing with U.S.-Asian relations with the Department of State, the Senate Foreign Relations Committee, and the CIA. Dr. Sutter received his Ph.D. in history and East Asian languages from Harvard University. He teaches regularly at Georgetown University and the University of Virginia and has published several books and articles dealing with contemporary China and Japan and their relations with the United States.

Chapter 1

INTRODUCTION: CHINA'S THIRD WORLD ROLE

by Lillian Craig Harris and Robert L. Worden

China has no doubts about its Third World credentials. On every appropriate occasion, whether greeting a developing nation's head of state, reporting to the National People's Congress, or addressing the UN General Assembly, Beijing's leaders and spokesmen unambiguously assert that China is a member of the Third World. According to one authoritative Chinese statement, not only does China belong to the Third World because it "has shared the same historical experience with other Third World nations," but "strengthening [its] unity and cooperation with other Third World nations is [China's] basic foreign policy."[1]

Yet despite this confident Chinese claim to Third World membership, it is easy to find those (invariably non-Chinese) who are not so sure. They point out that when testing various definitions of the Third World—itself an unsatisfactory and frustrating semantic exercise—China can be found among the low-income nations, but ranking well above other developing nations in per capita GNP, GNP growth rate, physical quality of life, life expectancy, literacy and public education, and military expenditures. China is also well below Third World averages for birth and death rates, does not share the direct colonial occupation experience of many Third World states, and unlike most developing countries, is an extremely large country blessed with a variety of development resources. Where then the similarity?[2]

1

The answer, of course, is that China is part of the Third World because China assigns itself to that amorphous group. There is no clear definition of "Third World"—a political term that has come to mean those developing and less-industrialized countries opposed to political and economic domination by the superpowers and the developed world. Identification with this concept is useful to China. It should be remembered, however, that an identity that is chosen can also be rejected. Might China someday decide it is not a part of the Third World?

History of China's Third World Position

The People's Republic of China was well represented at the symbolic founding of the Third World coalition at Bandung, Indonesia, in 1955. There was disagreement even at this point, however, on how China's nonaligned credentials measured up. Some Bandung participants agreed that both China and the Soviet Union—then ostensibly still closely cooperating with each other— were closer in outlook to the nonaligned states than to the Western countries which still had colonial holdings in Africa. Others believed that China was closer to the developed nations because of its immense population and potential national power.

Indeed, during the early 1950s, following long-standing Maoist principles, China rejected the concept of nonalignment, or neutralism, as reactionary. Chinese leaders tended to share U.S.S.R. and U.S. attitudes that, despite massive aid programs to the Third World, there was little cause for optimism. By 1954, however, Chinese thinking had changed and the Third World was seen as a weapon that could be used against the United States and the ever-distancing Soviet Union. At the First National People's Congress in 1954, Zhou Enlai announced the Five Principles of Peaceful Coexistence[3] as the basis of Chinese foreign policy and recognized the positive role of developing world "national bourgeoise leaders" in the anti-imperialist movement.

From that time onward, China has consistently identified itself with the Third World—despite broad policy swings during the 1960s and 1970s. The so-called "Bandung Era" from 1954 to 1959 was a time of intense Chinese effort to influence the Third World through diplomatic maneuvers. But as the 1950s drew to a close, China had become more aggressive in its actions and rigid in its political philosophies, alienating many of its former Third World friends. The 1960s began and ended with Chinese confrontationism in foreign policy; China has not yet entirely recovered from the damage done to its international image in that era. Third World nations are not all convinced of China's peaceful intentions.

In the mid-1960s, in almost a perverse foreshadowing of present "independent" foreign policy, Beijing rejected both "revisionism" and "imperialism," both the Soviet Union and the United States, seeking instead to promote opposition to the two superpowers and to encourage "revolution" wherever possible. By 1968 the Cultural Revolution was in full swing, China's foreign as well as domestic policies were in chaos, and relations with many other countries, including many in the Third World, had been severely strained.

The Cultural Revolution had actually very little to do with the Third World, despite spillovers of Chinese violence to other countries. Defense Minister Lin Biao's famous ode to political violence, "Long Live the Victory of People's War," instead of being a battle cry for export of revolution—as many feared—was really a Chinese warning to Third World countries, North Vietnam in particular, that they must rely on their own resources in the battle against imperialism and not expect China to bail them out. A transitional period in Chinese foreign policy from 1969 to 1971 followed perceptions of increased threat from the Soviet Union and eventually led to normalization of diplomatic ties with the United States.

In all this the Third World figured very little. What should be clear, however, is the major role which both the United States and the Soviet Union have always played in China's foreign policies. Since creation of the People's Republic of China in 1949, Beijing's relationship with the two superpowers has been the strongest determinant in China's foreign policy direction. This situation is likely to continue. China's efforts to position itself as a Third World leader can be interpreted in light of the effort to find supporters in the quest for independence from superpower control—hence the current strong emphasis by China's leadership on Third World identity.

What China Wants

But China's identification with the Third World is also rooted in China's self-image, national aspirations, and world view. Modern Chinese attitudes and policies of political and cultural defensiveness, economic conservatism, and self-reliance have both historical and cultural roots. Experience of foreign encroachment and past Chinese humiliation combine with a traditional preference for self-reliance and a cultural concept of Chinese superiority to prevent China from easily trusting other states or dealing with them on an equal basis.

China is, in fact, still fighting its way out of centuries of isolation, still deciding how it can maintain its security and "Chineseness" while implementing an apparently necessary integration into the international community. Despite the notions of some outsiders to the contrary, China's foreign policy continues to be propelled by national interests rather than ideology. Identification with the Third World contributes toward achievement of those basic Chinese goals that do not change under successive leaderships: achievement of national security and international recognition of China's rightful position of prominence and authority.

Broadly interpreted, in the 1980s this means national modernization, good relations with potentially threatening outsiders, and acceptance by other countries of a major international role for China. Yet none of these goals has much to do with the Third World except in a negative sense. For modernization assistance China must turn to the developed world and enter into financial competition with the Third World. For secure borders it must ameliorate tensions with both superpowers, seeking to strike a balance between them. (It is important that there is no significant triangular relationship among any other Third World state and the United States and the Soviet Union, another factor raising questions about China's true identity.) Yet this very dependence on seeking balance limits China's freedom of action.

China as Third World "Leader"

Criticism of Mao's mistakes following his death in 1976 has not included rejection of his famous theory differentiating the three worlds.[4] China has continued to cling to that doctrine, although it has been subject to considerable reinterpretation. The present emphasis on an "independent" foreign policy has brought a revival of appeals to the Five Principles of Peaceful Coexistence, a set of principles in conflict with the violence called for by the Three Worlds Theory.

In the 1980s, China preaches a dual message of self-reliance and the need for Third World unity against the superpowers. "International duty" contrasts with its own relative inability to provide the kind of assistance needed in the Third World due to China's low level of development. China does not, however, advocate violence or "people's war" except in specially selected circumstances, as pointed out in Chapter 7. But the importance of the doctrine of people's war as a foreign policy tool is illustrated by China's promotion of that notion in two of the three situations cited by China as obstacles to normalization of Sino-Soviet relations: Soviet presence in Afghanistan and Vietnamese presence in Kampuchea. China's foreign policy of peaceful coexistence with the Third World is actually a convenient counterpoint to its policies toward the superpowers.

Champion or Challenger?

China presents itself as a rallying point for Third World unity and Third World efforts to receive a fair share of international power and economic benefit. Authoritative Chinese sources have stated strongly that China's veto power on the UN Security Council "represents the Third World"—despite the fact that since the People's Republic was seated in the United Nations in 1971, it has almost never used that veto to promote Third World causes. Security Council membership provides China with a sort of "power of attorney" for the Third World. But it also provides grist to those who question whether China is really a member of the Third World or actually a great power.

Moreover, despite efforts to identify closely with the Third World, China continues to resist more active involvement in Third World affairs: It is not a member of the two major Third World organizations, the politically motivated Non-Aligned Movement and the economically oriented Group of 77. Nor has it chosen a significant leadership role in any of the international organizations which service Third World demands and needs. Some view this phenomenon as proof that the Chinese have never gotten completely away from the Confucian ideal of China as a model, in this case a model to the developing world of national unity, political development, and resistance to superpower domination.

Despite all its efforts to influence the developing nations, China claims to believe that the Third World needs no leader. On a number of occasions China has, in fact, vigorously denied that it aspires to Third World leadership: All Third World countries are political equals that can discuss and solve their problems in the spirit of unity and mutual assistance and therefore have no need for leader-follower relationships. Clearly, however, China sees itself as an adviser and facilitator to the Third World, a sort of political elder-brother posture which in fact places China in a superior position.

Thus, despite China's arguments about unity with the Third World, there are compelling factors hindering that unity. Lack of active involvement in the Third World, as opposed to rhetorical support, is only one of these. Growing competition with the Third World for markets and for available international development funds does not augur well for closer Chinese–Third World ties. But perhaps most important is that the same political and ideological forces that keep Beijing from becoming too closely aligned with either the Soviet Union or the United States have also prevented it from forging too close a relationship with the Third World. China's underlying drive to act in an independent manner—the "independent" foreign policy officially adopted at the Twelfth Party Congress in 1982—continues to act against close Chinese cooperation or coordination with any group, including the Third World.

Points of Conflict and Complement

China's efforts to assert influence in the Third World are tied to other constraints as well. To achieve international recognition of China's special position—which, in Beijing's view, clearly includes a prominent leadership role in Asia—is to raise the concerns of China's Third World neighbors. The *Asian Third World has a special relationship with China* due to long historical contact, large overseas Chinese communities, and economic issues, all situations rooted in geographic proximity. It is doubtful that any nation the size of China could survive for long other than as primus inter pares among nations the size of most Asian states. Asians, Southeast Asians in particular, are concerned by this truth.

China's special relationship with its Asian neighbors is not only a constraint on China's freedom of action in the Third World. It is a danger area where a misstep could give cause for significant opposition to China on a variety of issues. If China truly intends to achieve a position of Third World authority, the Asian Third World must be "on China's side." More importantly, a significant Asian leadership role for China depends on good ties with the small Asian nations.

Inability to compete with the developed nations in supplying aid to the Third world restricts China's ability to influence some developing states, particularly in Africa. Nonetheless, China has a good record for "no strings attached" aid and continues to provide assistance where it can. A vigorous foreign aid program begun in the 1950s reached a high point in the 1960s but was scaled back in the 1970s due to the emphasis on China's own internal development needs. The interesting point here is that provision of aid and experts to other countries is more characteristic of great power behavior than of the relationship of one developing country to another.

China's uncertainty over its role in international organizations is a serious restriction to China's Third World position. Failure to move toward more active involvement in international groups reflects in part the failure of China's aggressive efforts in the 1950s and 1960s to assume control of various Third World organizations such as the Afro-Asian People's Solidarity Organization. However, such apparent passivity has also raised the question of the extent of China's actual commitment to Third World causes—and thus by extention China's true identity.

Perspectives on China's Third World Policy

A key judgment made by Robert Sutter in Chapter 2 is that, at best, Third World policy plays a secondary role in China's approach to foreign affairs. Economic modernization, as well as traditional concerns for national defense and internal security, weigh heavier in the formulation of global policy. China's foreign policy is, in fact, more focused on the superpowers and the developed world than on Third World issues. Close Chinese ideological identity with Third World issues will not mean a turning away from what is most important to Chinese security and development: stable relations with the First and Second Worlds.

Nonetheless, the issues of U.S.S.R. world and regional dominance and the U.S. role in Asia are seen by Sutter as crucial ingredients affecting Beijing's Third World outlook. Part of China's deterrent and defensive strategies is to foster multifront opposition to the Soviet Union in the Second and Third Worlds. A stable Asia-Pacific region, with hopes for diminished activity by the Soviet Union and the proper balancing presence of the United States, becomes a more critical imperative than Third World issues beyond China's periphery. The Third World countries of Asia are, therefore, the most important to China, as they play a direct and important role in Chinese security and economic development. Areas farther away are important mainly as stages to offset and balance China's anti-Soviet and implicitly pro-Western policies.

Carol Lee Hamrin takes up the critical question of foreign policy as an extension of domestic policy, concluding that the post-Mao leadership is characterized by a greater acceptance of the status quo in international affairs. She views this as the logical evolutionary stage resulting from the complex development of domestic and foreign factors facing China since World War II. Hamrin discusses the role of ideology in foreign policy in the context of Mao Zedong's Three Worlds Theory, itself the result of an evolutionary view of the developing world and China's place in it. After reviewing the history of this evolution, she turns to an analysis of the key factors affecting the mid-1980s emergence of China's "new 'peace' paradigm." China's advocacy of peace—an essential requirement for continuity and success in China's domestic modernization program—is seen as even more salient than other foreign policy themes, including independence, antihegemony, and Third World unity. Hamrin argues that the mid-1980s emergence of a Chinese "one world market" doctrine will have a dramatic effect on Third World policy as China's leaders align foreign and domestic trends in terms of coexistence between capitalism and socialism at home and abroad.

In her essay on China's Third World policy as a counterpoint to the United States and the Soviet Union, Sarah-Ann Smith takes up the theme of the relative importance to China of the various parts of the Third World. She argues, however, that Beijing's policy toward the developing world "is far more than a side issue in . . . [its] relationships to the two superpowers. . . . It is in fact a set of concepts which define the parameters of those relationships." Smith sees the expanding level of China's relationships with the superpowers not as negating the importance of China's Third World policy but, if anything, as making it more significant.

Smith also asks whether China's Third World policy is consistent with past practice and, in light of the importance of the superpowers to China's foreign policy goals, whether this policy really matters. Her answers are in the affirmative, although she explains that consistency does not mean identical practice. China's Third World policy, she concludes, has evolved as China itself has evolved, and domestic modernization needs will continue to drive foreign policy evolution.

Robert Worden examines China's championship of Third World causes in international organizations, arguing that China uses these groups as a major forum for projecting its own views on development, North-South relations, South-South cooperation, disarmament, decolonization, and other issues of vital concern to the developing world. As the People's Republic legitimized its place in global affairs, it made a quantum leap in its memberships, and thus in its voice, in international organizations, especially in the post-Mao era. Beijing is conscious of its national self-interests and is unlikely to compromise them for the sake of hallowed Third World principles. Instead, China's representatives have adopted a conservative modus operandi which balances criticisms of the First and Second Worlds with Beijing's own search for development assistance and the protection of international conventions.

Despite, in China's view, the importance of international organizations in Third World affairs, the key role the Third World plays in them, and Beijing's own moral support for numerous Third World regional organizations, China has not joined the preeminent Third World groups, the formal Non-Aligned Movement and the Group of 77. Moreover, Third World scepticism is raised by China's participation in such "old international economic order" establishments as the World Bank and the International Monetary Fund, which put China into direct competition for assistance with Third World nations. Third World wariness has also been raised by China's continued anti-Soviet rhetoric. The net result is growing conflict in China's Third World policy toward the international organizations.

Bruce Larkin describes the economic choices raised for the Third World by China as it becomes more heavily engaged in world trade, arguing that long-range effects will follow from Beijing's modernization initiatives. Leaving aside the question of whether China's economic competition is "good" or "bad," Larkin asks if Chinese participation will change the economic choices of

Third World states. His conclusion is that Chinese commercial and economic activism in the Third World will leave developing countries with a greater array of Chinese material and technological products, but present them with competition for supply of other commodities available elsewhere in the Third World. He projects, too, greater competition between China and other developing nations for loans and services from the international banking community as well as from other international organizations. Political tension will arise from this heightened economic interplay, with the earliest manifestations likely to come in Southeast Asia.

Lillian Craig Harris concludes that although people's war wears a new guise and is seldom mentioned, it remains very much alive. China continues to employ the concept as a political tool and is unlikely to abandon such a useful doctrine in the near future. The importance of people's war for China's foreign, including Third World, policy is illustrated by Chinese promotion of the concept in an attempt to force Soviet compliance in two of the three situations cited by China as obstacles to normalization of Sino-Soviet relations: the Soviet occupation of Afghanistan and the Vietnamese occupation of Kampuchea. In addition to use of people's war to keep pressure on the Soviet Union, however, China's moderate leadership also employs the concept to underscore its revolutionary credentials, both abroad and in catering to the desires of the generally more conservative Chinese military. The concept also provides for continued support to "old friends" in Southeast Asia while allowing a potential means of pressure on regional governments. Harris concludes, however, that Third World suspicions, particularly on the part of China's Asian neighbors, of China's ultimate intentions are reinforced by failure of the People's Republic to renounce the doctrine of people's war, no matter how useful it may remain to China.

Robert Manning's chapter deals with developing world reactions to China's Third World policy and describes the mixture of praise, admiration, criticism, and scepticism that Third World nations exhibit toward China. Manning finds that Beijing's post-Mao approaches to the Third World have generally been well received in the Third World, most notably in Africa, where China has aggressively asserted its nonaligned posture and has granted relatively large amounts of aid. He sees, however, more narrow Chinese interests at work in the Third World regions on China's periphery (Northeast, South, and Southeast Asia), while in other regions (the

Middle East and Latin America) China's role is marginal. Although Manning believes Beijing's foreign policy is generally accepted at face value, he argues that "the absence of any public criticism of China's self-aggrandizing behavior appears to reflect local fears of alienating Beijing and an appreciation for China's diplomatic support in international fora." As the 1980s proceed, moreover, the competitive nature of China–Third World relations is likely to emerge, although it will possibly be balanced by Beijing's support of nonaligned positions in North-South competition.

Prognosis

The future of China's relationship with the Third World remains uncertain, although China's self-identification with that group will almost certainly continue well into the 21st century. Because it is difficult to define the Third World and because Chinese policy is so clearly driven, as it must be, by China's own national concerns, China's Third World relations will undoubtedly depend more and more on individual relations with Third World states. This is not, essentially, a new phenomenon. But China's need to deal separately with Third World nations, to come out from the refuge of an umbrella Third World policy, will become increasingly clear as the points of conflict between China and Third World countries develop unevenly—as they are bound to do.

Even the dichotomy between relations with the Third World as a whole and with its individual members is in itself a source of potential conflict. The essence of third worldliness lies in commonality of historical experience and in aspirations for unified action. In this sense, the Third World has significance only when it coalesces—ideally globally but at least regionally—in international organizations. Any Chinese policy or action perceived, wrongfully or not, as smacking of an effort to divide and conquer will come under the closest scrutiny by foreign observers.

In the remaining years of this century, the dominant factor in China's foreign relations will remain Chinese domestic politics. Moreover, as has been true since 1949, China's relations with the superpowers will remain the major external determinant of China's policy. Much of the Third World already recognizes the phenomenon of a China limited by self-interest and by its ties to the superpowers, despite the claim to an independent foreign policy. But the developing world has not yet accepted the truth that China's post-1982 "independent" foreign policy requires that China remain in many senses independent from the Third World itself. China's size, Security Council seat, and ability to manipulate the great powers keep alive developing world hopes that China will emerge as a champion for Third World causes. Yet during the next few years, China will find Third World demands increasingly at variance with its national objectives and needs. As this occurs, and as the Chinese challenge to Third World economic and political objectives becomes more evident, China's Third World identity will increasingly be called into question by Third World states themselves.

Endnotes

1. "Ten Questions in Foreign Relations," *Banyue Tan* (Beijing), May 10, 1984, p. 14, as translated in Foreign Broadcast Information Service, *Daily Report: China*, June 11, 1984, p. A3.
2. For further discussion on China's place in the Third World, cf.: George Thomas Kurian, *Encyclopedia of the Third World* (New York: Facts on File, 1978), 2 vols.; William P. Raynall, *Dictionary of Politics, Selected American and Foreign Political and Legal Terms* (Lawrenceville, Va.: Brunswick Publishing, 1978); and Gwyneth Williams, *Third-World Political Organizations, A Review of Developments* (Montclair, N.J.: Allanheld, Osmum, 1981). Also see Robert Cassen et al., *Rich Country Interests and Third World Development* (New York: St. Martin's Press, 1982), various pages; Christopher Clapham, *Third World Politics: An Introduction* (Madison: University of Wisconsin Press, 1985), pp. 1–4; Pradip K. Ghosh (editor), *New International Economic Order: A Third World Perspective* (Westport, Conn.: Greenwood Press, 1984), pp. xvii and 556–568; Sanjaya Lall, *Developing Countries in the International Economy* (London: Macmillan Press, Ltd., 1981), p. 164; Robert A. Mortimer, *The Third World Coalition in International Politics* (Boulder and London: Westview Press, 1984), p. 1; and Michael P. Todaro, *Economic Development in the Third World* (New York and London: Longman, 1985), p. 610.
3. The Five Principles are mutual respect for sovereignty and territorial integrity, mutual nonaggression, noninterference in each other's internal affairs, equality and mutual benefit, and peaceful coexistence.
4. The "Theory of the Differentiation of the Three Worlds" can be summarized as follows: "Basically, Mao divided the world into three spheres: the First World of the two superpowers, the United States and the USSR; the Second World essentially comprising the developed world of Europe and Japan; and the Third World, whose membership includes both socialist countries and the oppressed, underdeveloped nations. Mao described the Third World as 'the

main force in the worldwide struggle against imperialism and hegemonism' and said that, although the Second World oppresses and exploits the Third, it is itself 'controlled and bullied by the superpowers.' This contradiction can be exploited by the Third World to win over the Second and unite with it in the common struggle for self-determination." See Lillian Craig Harris, *Washington Papers, China's Foreign Policy Toward the Third World* (Washington, D.C.: Center for Strategic and International Studies, Georgetown University, No. 112, 1985), p. 3.

Chapter 2

STRATEGIC AND ECONOMIC IMPERATIVES AND CHINA'S THIRD WORLD POLICY

by Robert G. Sutter

China's policy toward the Third World is not formulated in a vacuum. It has long been heavily influenced by broader Chinese policy concerns. Thus, even though Chinese spokesmen repeatedly have maintained that support for Third World concerns remains at the center of Chinese foreign policy, careful examination of the record over the past decade shows that such concerns at best have a secondary role to play in determining China's 1980s approach to foreign affairs. The examination shows that China's foreign policy is based primarily on its perceived need for stability, security, and development, a policy that depends chiefly on China's relations with the United States and the Soviet Union. Nevertheless, China does retain a strong interest in maintaining an image of close identification with the developing countries and has demonstrated a tendency to do so whenever it will support, or at least not seriously jeopardize, its primary needs of stability, security, and development.

Determinants of Recent Chinese Foreign Policy[1]

The objectives of recent Chinese foreign policy are determined by top-level Chinese leaders who reflect the broad interests of the

14

Chinese state, as well as their own parochial ambitions. In the past, Mao Zedong, Zhou Enlai, and other senior leaders exerted overriding control over foreign policy. In recent years, the number of officials involved in advising about Chinese foreign policy has increased, yet key decisions remain the preserve of a small group of leaders, especially Deng Xiaoping.

The primary concerns of these leaders have not focused on support for the Third World; they have focused on efforts to guarantee Chinese national security, maintain internal order, and pursue economic development. Especially since the death of Mao in 1976, the top priority of Chinese leaders has been to promote successful economic modernization. This development represents the linchpin determining the success or failure of their leadership. Thus, Chinese officials have geared China's foreign policy to help the modernization effort.

Creating a Stable Regional Environment

In order to accomplish economic modernization, as well as to maintain national security and internal order, Chinese leaders recognize the fundamental prerequisite of establishing a relatively stable strategic environment, especially around China's periphery in Asia. The alternative would be a highly disruptive situation requiring much greater Chinese expenditures on national defense and posing greater danger to Chinese domestic order and tranquility. Unfortunately for China, it does not control this environment. It has influenced it, but the environment remains controlled more by others, especially the superpowers and their allies and associates. As a result, China's leaders have been required repeatedly to assess their surroundings for changes that could affect Chinese security and development interests. And they have been compelled repeatedly to adjust foreign policy to take account of such changes.

Nationalistic and Ideological Objectives

At the same time, Chinese leaders also have nationalistic and ideological objectives regarding irredentist claims (Taiwan, for example) and a desire to stand independently in foreign affairs as a leading force among "progressive" nations of the Third World. Politically, these goals have struck a responsive chord inside China. Occasional leadership discussion and debate over these and other questions regarding foreign affairs, including developments in the Third World, have sometimes had an effect on the course of Chinese foreign policy. In the past Maoist period, for example, Chinese leaders sometimes allowed these nationalistic and ideological objectives and other questions of political debate to jeopardize seriously the basic security and developmental interests of the Chinese state. China's move toward greater pragmatism in foreign and domestic policy since the late 1960s was not developed smoothly; it was often accompanied by very serious leadership debates over which foreign policy goals should receive priority. However, since the early 1970s, the debates have become progressively less acrimonious, and the foreign policy differences raised in these debates have become more moderate and less of a challenge to the recent dominant objectives of national development and security.

Thus, China's top foreign policy priority has remained the pragmatic quest for a stable environment essential to effective modernization and development. Since 1969 Chinese leaders have seen the main danger as negative change in the surrounding environment posed by the Soviet Union. At first, China saw Soviet power as an immediate threat to its national security. Over time, it came to see the Soviet Union as more of a long-term threat, determined to use its growing military power and other sources of influence to encircle and pressure China into accepting a balance of influence in Asia dominated by the Soviet Union and contrary to Chinese interests.

China's Soviet Strategy

China's strategy against the Soviet threat has been both bilateral and global. Bilaterally, China has used a mix of military preparations and tactical political moves to keep the Soviets from attacking China, but without compromising China's basic security interests. Globally, China's strategy has focused on developing either implicitly or explicitly an international united front designed to halt Soviet expansion and prevent the consolidation of Soviet dominance abroad.

The U.S. Counterweight

As the most important international counterweight to Soviet power, the United States has loomed large in Chinese calculations.

As the United States, under terms of the Nixon Doctrine announced in 1969, seemed determined to withdraw from its past containment policy in Asia and thereby ended the perceived American threat to China's national security, China was prepared to start the process of Sino-American normalization. The process has been complemented in recent years by China's enhanced interest in pragmatic economic modernization, which has emphasized the importance of technical and financial help from the West and access to Western markets.

Closer Chinese ties with the United States continue to be complicated by Chinese nationalistic and ideological concerns over such issues as Taiwan and Third World questions, as well as by fundamental differences between the social, political, and economic systems of the United States and China. Most notably, U.S. support for Taiwan is seen as a continued affront to China's sense of national sovereignty. But Chinese leaders have differentiated between substantive threats to their security, posed by the Soviet Union, as opposed to threats to their ideological sense of national sovereignty, posed by U.S. support for Taiwan.

In short, China has worked hard, and continues to work hard, to ensure that its strategic environment, threatened mainly by Soviet expansion, remains stable, so that China can focus on its economic modernization. China sees the Soviet Union as having a strategy of expansion that uses military power relentlessly but cautiously in order to achieve political influence and dominance throughout the periphery of the Soviet Union. China has long held that the focus of Soviet attention is in Europe, but that NATO's strength requires Moscow to work in other areas, notably the Middle East, Southwest Asia, Africa, and East Asia in order to outflank the Western defenses. China is seen as relatively low on Moscow's list of military priorities, although Chinese leaders clearly appreciate the dire consequences for China should the Soviet Union be able to consolidate its position elsewhere and then focus its strength to intimidate China.

China's strategy of deterrence and defense, therefore, aims basically to exacerbate Soviet defense problems by enhancing the worldwide opposition to Soviet expansion in general, and by raising the possibility of the Soviet Union confronting a multifront conflict in the event it attempted to attack or intimidate China in particular. Chinese leaders see China's cooperation with the United States as especially important in strengthening deterrence of the Soviet Union and in aggravating Soviet strategic vulnerabilities. Beijing also encourages anti-Soviet efforts by so-called Second World, developed countries, most of whom are formal allies of the United States, and by developing countries of the Third World. At the same time, Beijing uses a mix of political talks, bilateral exchanges, and other forms of dialogue to help manage the danger posed by the Soviet Union.

Domestic Determinants

Meanwhile, within this overall strategy to establish a stable environment in Asia, Chinese leaders have employed a varying mix of tactics to secure their interests. Tactics depend on international variables, such as the perceived strength and intentions of the superpowers, and Chinese domestic variables, such as the status of leadership cohesion or disarray. For example, when Chinese leaders have judged that their strategic surroundings were at least temporarily stable, they have seen less immediate need for close ties with the United States and thus have felt more free to adopt strident policies on Taiwan, Third World questions, and other nationalist issues that appeal to domestic constituencies but offend the United States. (This type of logic was in part responsible for China's tougher approach toward the United States over Taiwan, Central America, and other issues from 1981 to 1983.) When the Chinese leaders have judged that such tactics could seriously alienate the United States and thereby endanger the stability of China's environment, however, they have put them aside in the interests of preserving peaceful surroundings. (This kind of logic was in part responsible for China's moderation in approach toward the United States in 1983 and 1984.)

Also, Chinese domestic developments and leadership debate over foreign policy, while not the immediate determinants in China's foreign policy, help to explain recent tactical shifts in China's approach to foreign affairs. In particular, it is noted that some leaders in China may prefer a foreign policy truly independent of both the Soviet Union and the United States, one more closely identifying China with the Third World; circumstances at home and aboard at times may push Chinese foreign policy tactics in this direction. But, such temporary and marginal shifts are unlikely to lead to a basic change in China's overall foreign strategy, at least for some time to come; China's weakness in influencing its Asian surroundings, the steady buildup of Soviet pressure in Asia, and the implicitly positive role the United States continues to play for basic Chinese security and development interests continue to require a Chinese strategy of tilting closer to the West against the Soviet Union.

Implications for Chinese Policy in the Third World

The implications of this overall foreign policy framework for Chinese policy in the Third World appear clear. China's concern with Third World issues, outside of China's periphery in Asia, has been *secondary*. In effect, Chinese policy in these areas has represented a relatively small tail being wagged by a very large dog representing China's quest for a stable environment and effective modernization. This pattern of Chinese policies in the Third World generally following the direction set by Chinese security and development concerns is seen in the various tactical changes that have taken place in Chinese policy toward the Third World since the early 1970s.

After a period of fundamental reassessment in Chinese foreign policy in the late 1960s, China adopted a strategy designed to manage menacing Soviet power through Sino-Soviet border talks, Chinese defense preparations, and expanded international contacts, especially with the United States. As part of its greater international activity at this time, Beijing strove to broaden political contacts with Third World and other countries. It attempted to use such contacts to pursue the prevalent foreign policy interests of the Chinese state. Thus, while Chinese leaders continued to attack U.S. policy on various Third World issues, they clearly differentiated between the two superpowers and focused the bulk of their rhetoric against Moscow. This was particularly the case whenever Chinese officials saw the Soviet Union behind developments affecting Chinese security concerns in Asia, such as the alleged Soviet role in support of India against Pakistan in 1971. Other Chinese pronouncements strongly identified China with the bulk of Third World opinion on such issues as decolonization, apartheid, Palestinian rights, and a new international economic order. More controversially, they also attempted to defend China's growing nuclear arsenal against Third World and other criticism, to disparage growing international concern with environmental pollution—

seeing such concern as a scheme by the developed nations to hamper Third World development—and to support strongly the OPEC oil cartel.

A Chinese perceived shift in the East-West balance of power occurred in the mid-1970s. Beijing saw U.S. resolve against the Soviet Union weaken as a result of the Watergate crisis, the Western economic recession, and the Indochina debacle, and it worried about what it saw in the United States and the West as a "trend toward appeasement" of the expansionist Soviets. It saw this trend particularly in the U.S.-Soviet summit at Vladivostok in 1974 and the Helsinki summit in 1975. It also focused on the perceived danger of the Soviet Union taking advantage of changes in Africa (for example, Angola), East Asia (Vietnam, for example), and elsewhere in the developing world in order to expand its influence in competition with the West. But China could do little on its own in response. It was racked by serious internal crises, capped by a major leadership transition that removed by death or purge over half of China's ruling elite in a two-year period. As a result, Chinese officials were constrained to focus on rhetorical warnings to the West and the Third World. Based on China's unique interpretation of Lenin's theory of imperialism, they stressed the rising "danger of war" posed by the late-coming "Soviet social-imperialism."

As Deng Xiaoping began to consolidate his power in 1977 and 1978, Beijing took more active measures to establish an "antihegemony international front" with the Third World and other countries against the Soviet Union. Highlights included sharp condemnations of the Kremlin and its alleged Third World proxies, expecially Cuba and Vietnam, for their expansion in Africa and Indochina. Chinese pronouncements also began to softpedal past ideologically based identity with the Third World and underlined Chinese economic needs for modernization, which required a substantial cutback in Chinese aid donations to developing countries. The high point of China's anti-Soviet approach in the Third World was seen in Beijing's attack against Vietnam early in 1979, following the Vietnamese invasion of China's protege, Kampuchea.

The results of China's military lesson against Vietnam were mixed. In particular, Vietnam managed to return tit-for-tat and received ample support from its Soviet ally to offset Chinese pressure.

These setbacks added to growing international and domestic pressures on Deng Xiaoping and his reform-minded associates. Particularly repressive were increased Soviet military and political pressure around China's periphery and temporary setbacks in Chinese economic modernization and political reform at home. In response, Chinese leaders discussed and debated foreign policy options and decided to initiate several tactical adjustments in China's approach to foreign affairs. These included the start of Sino-Soviet negotiations, at least ostensibly designed to improve bilateral relations; the decline in China's heretofore outspoken interest in identifying closely with the United States on a strategic plane against the Soviet Union; and greater Chinese willingness to broaden political ties and other contacts with a variety of Third World governments, international political movements, and international Communist parties heretofore shunned as unhelpful or antagonistic to China's anti-Soviet objectives. Despite such alterations, however, Chinese actions and policy pronouncements made amply clear that Beijing's tactical adjustments were still focused on the basic Chinese need to stabilize the Asian environment in the face of Soviet pressure. Strategic means included effective, pragmatic diplomacy; reliance on continued, strong international opposition, especially U.S. opposition, to Moscow; and the maintenance of common Sino-American understanding against suspected Soviet designs in Asia.

Revived Interest in the Third World

Coincident with the tactical shift seen in China's posture toward the superpowers in the wake of the 1979 Chinese military incursion into Vietnam, Beijing came increasingly to see its past strident, anti-Soviet stress in the Third World as counterproductive, and China began to readjust that policy. The result over the next few years, as a key element in Beijing's portrayal of a more independent image in foreign affairs, was a slow but steady reemphasis on greater Chinese interest in fostering better relations with the developing countries. Beijing was nonetheless careful to ensure that this kind of image building and search for tactical advantage did not jeopardize China's concern to achieve stability around its frontiers. Thus, China appeared to use its "independence" from the United States and the West in areas more peripheral to basic Chinese security and development concerns, such as Latin America and Africa, as a means to offset and balance the continued anti-Soviet and implicitly pro-Western thrust of Chinese policy in much more important Third World areas for China, such as Southeast Asia.

Of course, Beijing had long held that China was a member of the Third World and that the developing countries were a vital force in the international struggle against the "hegemony" of the super-powers. In the initial period following Deng's return to power, Beijing had been quite strident in fostering political opposition to expansion of Soviet influence among the developing countries. Following a strategy of working with established Third World governments, Beijing had continued previous efforts to put aside its earlier ties with more radical and divisive "revolutionary" groups there. In the Chinese lexicon, Beijing now followed a strategy of "united front from above" against the forces of imperialism and domination, as opposed to the past policy of "united front from below."[2]

In their strong efforts to build a common front against the Soviet Union in 1977 and 1978, Chinese officials and propaganda had often been ham-handed and, as a result, had alienated China from the main currents of thinking among many Third World leaders. Thus, a number of leaders in developing countries became increasingly suspicious of Chinese intentions as China put aside past differences with the United States and the West for the sake of Chinese strategic and economic advantage. These Third World officials became more susceptible to Soviet charges that China had "sold out" to imperialist and reactionary forces in its eager search for leverage against the Soviets. Indeed, the Chinese showed they were willing to cooperate with some of the most reactionary Third World governments, such as Chile's Pinochet regime, as long as they were suitably anti-Soviet. And Beijing not only sharply attacked Vietnam and Cuba as Soviet proxies, but privately criticized or shunned other states (for example, Syria, South Yemen, Mozambique) that were considered by China to be too beholden to the Soviet Union for economic aid or political support.

Coincidentally, China was keeping its new aid commitments to the developing countries to a minimum and began to show interest in competing with other developing countries for aid from international organizations and for access to Western markets.[3] Of course,

Beijing had good reasons for reducing its past, often generous, aid commitments to certain developing countries:

- China needed resources at home for the ambitious modernization program.
- Past Chinese aid commitments to Third World countries had often been poorly utilized. For example, the showpiece of Chinese aid in Africa, the TanZam Railway, did not run properly after being completed by China.
- Aid often fostered governments that turned against China. Vietnam and Albania were the most important examples of this trend; but other instances included the regimes in South Yemen and Mozambique, which received considerable support from China in the past only to turn to more pro-Soviet policies later on.
- Large amounts of Chinese aid to particular developing countries sometimes tended to prompt the Soviets to offer even greater aid in order to compete directly with China and overwhelm Chinese influence. As a result, China lost influence despite its past investment.

The combination of China's controversial pro-Western, anti-Soviet political orientation and its more niggardly aid effort diminished Chinese influence with many developing countries by 1979. In response, Chinese leaders, especially in the Ministry of Foreign Affairs and the CCP International Liaison Department, at that time began a series of low-keyed visits to Third World states as part of a reassessment of China's posture in this part of the world. Although China's renewed emphasis on policy independence and closeness to the developing world would not emerge full blown for two more years, by 1979 several signs of tactical change were already in evidence:

- Beijing began to moderate its past strident anti-Soviet rhetoric and to pull back from close public identification with some conservative Third World regimes merely because they were anti-Soviet.
- Unless basic Chinese security interests were directly affected, as they were in China's opposition to Vietnam, Beijing increasingly tried to avoid the limelight on controversial Third World issues. Questions such as the conflict over control of Western

Sahara, the civil war in Chad, the Ethiopian-Somalian conflict over contested border lands, and, later, the Iran-Iraq war found China increasingly taking a publicly neutral position. At the same time, Beijing continued to voice strong support for positions that enjoyed a broad consensus in the Third World, such as opposition to Israel and South Africa, support for liberation groups directed against them, and support for a more equitable international economic order.

- China used its scaled-down aid effort to build as much political goodwill as possible. Thus, Chinese aid efforts tended to focus on high-profile projects that were finished cheaply and quickly and had ample opportunities for favorable publicity. Typical examples were Chinese constructed sports stadiums and auditoriums and small Chinese health teams throughout Africa.

- Beijing began more pragmatically to exploit quietly Third World markets for Chinese economic advantage. China's growing trade with Africa and the Middle East, for example, remained heavily in China's favor, providing a major source of foreign exchange.[4] Moreover, the Chinese began efforts to use the lucrative Middle East arms market as a source of foreign exchange and for political advantage.[5]

- Beijing attempted to shore up its influence in the Third World through more extensive political and technical contacts. This not only involved the traditional methods of lavish Chinese entertainment for visiting Third World leaders, but also increased Chinese exchanges with representatives of political parties, labor groups, women's organizations, military officials, and other interest groups. These exchanges cost the Chinese little in monetary terms but were useful in building a broader base of political influence. They had the added benefit of deepening Chinese understanding of opinions in particular developing countries, so that Beijing could avoid alienating leaders or offending particular sensibilities as the Chinese pursued their broader foreign policy objectives. A highlight of Beijing's more ecumenical approach to contacts with political parties in developing countries was seen in then CCP International Liaison Department Deputy Director Wu Xueqian's visit to ten African countries in late 1979. This was followed in mid-1980 by a visit to several African and Middle Eastern countries by the director of that department, Ji Pengfei.

China's "Independent" Foreign Policy and the Third World

Although China's interest in the Third World was forced to take a lower priority as Beijing focused, in 1980, on encouraging a strong anti-Soviet reaction in the West to the Soviet invasion of Afghanistan in late 1979, it resumed later that year and reached a high point from 1981 to 1983 under the rubric of China's "independent" foreign policy. By 1981, China was increasingly assured by the international balance of forces that was developing in the wake of the Soviet invasion of Afghanistan. For the first time in almost a decade, Beijing saw an international balance evolving that was likely, at least temporarily, to hold at bay the threat of Soviet expansion. Moscow's ability to use military power to extend its influence was also seen as sapped by growing economic, political, and military problems the Soviet leaders faced both at home and abroad.[6]

Foreign Policy Adjustments

China adjusted its foreign approach tactically to accord better with these altered circumstances. It moved to a posture more independent of the United States, closer in rhetoric to the developing countries of the Third World, and less hostile to Moscow. In many respects, China's new tactics represented a logical follow-on to the policy initiatives undertaken in 1979 that had been put aside in favor of a stronger anti-Soviet, pro-Western approach in the immediate aftermath of the Soviet invasion of Afghanistan.

As China adopted a more sanguine view of the international balance against Soviet expansion, began efforts to ease bilateral tension with the Soviet Union, and distanced itself from the United States over Taiwan and other questions, Beijing was in a better position to develop and broaden its relations with the Third World. Thus, Beijing showed more concern over, and active interest in, Third World issues through propaganda coverage, international exchanges, leadership meetings, and actions in international organizations. China's increased attention to Asian, African, and Latin American issues stopped short of increased outlays of Chinese aid, however; Beijing tried to enhance its image and influence cheaply. Its economic interchange tended to be very hardheaded and focused in areas that made economic, as well as political, profits for China.

Repairing Third World Ties

Chinese leaders, especially those with long experience in dealings with the Third World such as foreign affairs specialists Ji Pengfei, Wu Xueqian, and He Ying, were well aware of the costs China was paying in relations with many developing countries as a result of its earlier tilt toward the United States and the West and strident opposition to the Soviet Union and its associates. As China brought its policy toward the superpowers more in balance and began to assert its "independence" in foreign affairs, these officials took the lead in reestablishing and broadening Chinese influence with the developing countries. They had several immediate reasons for pushing ahead:

- Criticism of China in the Third World was on the rise. In particular, China was seen as unreasonably antagonistic toward Third World countries that received extensive aid and political support from the Soviet bloc; but China was also seen as unwilling to offer compensating aid in its own right.[7]
- Beijing had now become an active member of international financial institutions and was competing with developing countries for development funds from abroad.[8]
- Beijing was demanding a greater share of the markets of developed countries—a demand that would be met largely by cutting back on the market share enjoyed by other Third World states.[9]
- China was vulnerable to charges that it served as a stalking horse for U.S. and Western interests against the Soviet Union in the Third World.
- Beijing's image suffered as a result of Chinese racial discrimination against African students in China, publicized in repeated incidents in China.
- Beijing was involved heavily in political support and economic aid in many Third World countries in the past. Without careful nurturing, this long-term investment could be lost.
- Stronger ties with the developing world would increase China's support in the United Nations and other international

forums on issues important to Chinese security and other interests (for example, Afghanistan, Kampuchea).

- A stronger Chinese emphasis on the Third World, including greater criticism of U.S. policies, not only enhanced China's image among developing countries but also drew the attention of U.S. policymakers to one of the "costs" of a deteriorating U.S.-China relationship.
- By winning the confidence of Third World governments through a more independent international posture and greater political support and interchange, when necessary Beijing would be able to exert influence more effectively against Moscow. Thus, by reestablishing contacts with such previously alienated states as Angola, Libya, Mozambique, South Yemen, Syria, and Ethiopia, China was better positioned to watch for openings that would allow for a reduction in these countries' dependence on the Soviet Union.
- Improved Chinese political relations allowed for an opening of favorable Chinese trade relations. In the case of the Middle East and Africa, for example, Chinese trade grew as new markets were opened; it remained highly favorable for China, resulting in a trade surplus of over one billion dollars in 1982.[10] China also used good political ties to open markets for its arms sales and to send tens of thousands of contract workers to the Middle East—both together provided over a billion dollars of foreign exchange for China each year during the early 1980s.[11]

In their rhetoric during 1981, Chinese officials began to reaffirm—after a hiatus of several years—China's identity with the Maoist Three Worlds Theory. In August 1981, the prominent journal *Liaowang* reiterated the Three Worlds Theory as a basis of Chinese foreign policy. The article's stress coincided with the June 1981 Eleventh CCP Central Committee Sixth Plenum, which had offered a positive assessment of Mao Zedong's contributions to Chinese foreign policy.[12]

New Identities with the Third World

Subsequently, Chinese leaders softpedaled any Maoist ideological rationale for Chinese foreign policy including the Three Worlds Theory, but Beijing asserted its identity with the Third World through other means. Later in 1981, for instance, China became more critical of alleged U.S. "hegemonic" actions in Central America. The Chinese stance contrasted with Beijing's position earlier in the year in support of U.S. actions in the region against potential Soviet expansion. Beijing also worked hard to identify with the Third World against the United States and the Soviet Union when, during UN Security Council deliberations in late 1981, it repeatedly blocked the U.S.-supported candidate for UN Secretary General, and when it strongly sided with Argentina in UN debate over the Malvinas war in 1982. At the Cancun summit meeting of October 1981, meanwhile, Premier Zhao stressed China's strong support for developing countries' demands for establishing a new international economic order, which was opposed by the United States and other developed countries.[13]

Zhao's trip to Mexico coincided with a series of high-level Chinese visits to previously slighted Third World areas. Thus, Foreign Minister Huang Hua, who accompanied Zhao, had traveled earlier in 1981 to several Latin American stops. Huang and Vice Foreign Minister Gong Dafei also traveled to five African countries during this period. Their trips followed the extensive visits to the region made by CCP delegations led by Wu Xueqian and Ji Pengfei in late 1979 and mid-1980, respectively.

A capstone of this effort was seen in Zhao's 1982–1983 tour of 11 African countries. Throughout the visit, Beijing was at pains to underline China's strong reassertion of its Third World credentials and its pullback from close public association with the developed countries—the United States in particular—and its more balanced posture toward both superpowers.

The Zhao trip, the first of its kind since Premier Zhou Enlai's swing through Africa in 1963–1964, included polite, low-keyed discussions with African leaders of varying political views. As Zhao refused to commit China to many new Chinese aid programs or outlays, the trip epitomized Beijing's high-profile, low-cost effort to improve its standing among developed countries. At most stops, Zhao charged that superpower rivalry was the main source of political and economic instability in Africa and the rest of the Third World. In an effort to eliminate African and other Third World countries' tendencies to associate Chinese policy with the United States and the West, Zhao singled out unpopular U.S. policy in the Middle East and southern Africa for criticism. At the same time, he avoided caustic references to either the United States or the

Soviet Union in public, presumably out of deference to his hosts' sensibilities.

Zhao's separate meetings with PLO Chief Yasir Arafat, representatives of the South-West African People's Organization (SWAPO), and leaders of the African National Congress (ANC) and the Pan-Africanist Congress (PAC) enabled him to demonstrate Beijing's support for "liberation" groups that enjoyed broad support in the region. This was done even though SWAPO and ANC heretofore had been relatively distant from China and close to the Soviet Union.

China's more balanced approach was complemented by Zhao's refusal to become drawn into controversy over issues that divided the region, including the civil war in Chad, the Western Sahara dispute between Morocco and Algeria, the Iran-Iraq war, and the disagreement between Ethiopia and Somalia over their disputed border. Beijing thus carefully tailored its statements of support with an eye toward maximizing political gain and minimizing the risk of alienating important regional actors.

At most of his stops, Zhao offered to conclude trade and economic cooperation agreements as China's contribution to economic development of Third World nations. These and other agreements emphasized joint investment in small projects that would have a fairly rapid and relatively high political impact as well as low cost. Indeed, in this regard, the most common Chinese assistance projects in Africa came to be sports stadiums and medical teams. Zhao, meanwhile, was careful to counsel his hosts against mechanically following the past Chinese mode of self-reliant economic development.

Concurrent trips by Chinese officials established closer ties between Chinese and Third World leaders with diverse interests and specialties. Thus, Beijing sent senior trade union, military, economic, trade, women's group, National People's Congress and other officials abroad to establish new contacts with their Third World counterparts. Meanwhile, Third World specialists like He Ying were sent on troubleshooting missions to reestablish closer ties with important developing governments heretofore alienated from China—these included Libya, Syria, Iraq, South Yemen, Ethiopia, and Angola.[14]

Beijing's more flexible and economically pragmatic approach to the Third World allowed China to garner major economic benefits, for instance, in the oil-rich Middle East. Trade in the region ran heavily in China's favor, as it did throughout most of the Third World. In 1981, China recorded a $6.1 billion trade surplus with the developing countries.[15]

Adjusting Superpower Policies, 1983–1985: Implications for the Third World

Consolidating Ties with the West

Changes in Chinese calculations, based largely on perceptions of shifts in the international balance of power affecting China, caused Beijing to adjust its independent approach to foreign affairs beginning in 1983. At bottom, Chinese leaders became increasingly concerned about the stability of China's surroundings in Asia at a time of unrelenting buildup in Soviet military and political pressure throughout China's periphery, and of serious and possibly prolonged decline in Chinese relations with the United States. They decided that the Chinese foreign policy tactics of the previous two years, designed to distance China from the policies of the United States and to moderate and improve relations with the Soviet Union, were less likely to safeguard the important Chinese security and development concerns affected by the stability of the Asian environment. They recognized in particular that Beijing would have to stop its pullback from the United States for fear of jeopardizing this link so important for maintaining China's security and development interests in the face of persisting Soviet pressure in Asia. Thus, in 1983 Beijing began to retreat from some of the tactical changes made in the previous two years under the rubric of China's independent approach to foreign affairs. The result was a substantial reduction in Chinese pressure on the United States over Taiwan and other issues; increased Chinese interest and flexibility in dealing with the Reagan administration and other Western countries across a broad range of economic, political, and security issues; and for a time, heightened Sino-Soviet antipathy.

Shifting Tactics Toward the Soviet Union

Once relations with the United States were on a firmer footing following President Reagan's visit to China in 1984 and his subsequent reelection as President, Beijing attempted to avoid a confrontation with Moscow and gain economic benefits. Thus, during the December 1984 visit to China of Soviet Deputy Prime Minister Ivan Arkhipov, China agreed to Soviet initiatives involving improving Sino-Soviet economic relations. The rise of a new Soviet leader, Mikhail Gorbachev, in early 1985 raised hopes for further movement in bilateral relations, although prospects appeared limited because of continued Sino-Soviet strategic rivalry in Asia, especially involving fighting in Kampuchea.

Throughout this period, Beijing tried strongly to nurture wherever possible the increased influence it had garnered by means of its independent posture in the Third World. As long as Soviet-backed expansion at China's expense in Asia remained in check, and China's relations with the United States remained steady, Beijing was prepared to strike out rhetorically against the policies of both superpowers, and thereby build China's image and influence with the Third World. Most notably, Beijing adjusted its line on U.S.-Soviet arms control efforts. Whereas China in the 1970s had disparaged such efforts as a means to check the "unbridled" arms buildup of the Soviet Union, Beijing now identified directly with Third World support for a negotiated limitation in the U.S.-Soviet arms race and criticized U.S. or Soviet efforts to develop new weapons and related technology.

In part, China's altered stance was based on security concerns. The Chinese were worried over what they increasingly saw as a stepped-up superpower arms race that in East Asia had led to a steady buildup of Soviet forces and a widening in the gap between Soviet and Chinese military capabilities. China hoped to focus on economic modernization and to avoid the increased defense spending needed to keep pace with the Soviet advances. In the interim, to avoid domination by Moscow, Beijing increasingly found itself forced to compromise, and to establish closer military ties, with the United States. Thus, the Chinese saw the East-West arms race entering a new stage of development that would leave China militarily further behind the United States and the Soviet Union and reduce Chinese leverage with both powers. The arms race threatened greater bipolarity in world politics, making it more difficult for China to steer an "independent" foreign policy course.

At the same time, a moderate antisuperpower line fit in well with contemporary Chinese image making in the Third World and elsewhere. Thus, Beijing's arms control proposal at the United Nations Conference on Disarmament in 1982, and at the UN

General Assembly in the following years, turned away from China's own nuclear ambitions and focused instead on calls for the two superpowers to stop all testing, research, and manufacture of new nuclear weapons and to agree to cut their stockpiles in half. Once the latter pledge was made, Beijing said it would be willing to attend a world disarmament conference. Beijing obviously had little expectation that its proposal would win approval, but it served to focus critical attention exclusively on the superpowers in a way that would please the broad ranks of the international peace movement.

Assessment

The 1980s record shows that China's approach to the Third World has been determined by broader Chinese foreign policy concerns. China continues to give top priority to security and development concerns, which will force Chinese leaders to focus paramount attention on Chinese relations with the Soviet Union, the United States, and the developed countries. Third World countries that appear most important to China are those that have a direct and important role to play in helping China secure its environment in Asia or in developing its economy. The others will be of secondary importance.

Nevertheless, China will likely continue to use the relatively inexpensive means of rhetorical support in international and Third World organizations and elsewhere, leadership visits, and modest aid allotments to foster an image of policy independence and affinity to the Third World. Such a posture serves to preserve long-standing Chinese political equities with Third World governments, enhances Chinese international political leverage vis-à-vis the United States and the Soviet Union, and opens the way for China to secure economic benefit through trade and exchanges with these states. Chinese leaders also have a continuing ideological need to identify closely with the developing world, though, as a consequence of Beijing's recently more pragmatic pursuit of wealth and power on the international scene, this ideological concern has lost much of its power in Chinese policy.

Endnotes

1. Background for this section and much of the rest of the chapter is contained in my book *Chinese Foreign Policy: Developments After Mao* (New York: Praeger Publishers, 1985). For a good background on differing views on determinants of Chinese foreign policy, see Harry Harding (editor), *China's Foreign Relations in the 1980s* (New Haven: Yale University Press, 1984).
2. For an excellent review of China's policy toward the Third World up to 1980, see Harry Harding, "China and the Third World: From Revolution to Containment," in Richard Solomon (editor), *The China Factor: Sino-American Relations and the Global Scene* (Englewood Cliffs, N.J.: Prentice-Hall, 1981).
3. For an assessment of Chinese foreign aid efforts, see U.S. Congress, Joint Economic Committee, *Allocation of Resources in the Soviet Union and China, 1983* (Washington: U.S. Government Printing Office, 1984).
4. For Chinese foreign trade issues, see U.S. Central Intelligence Agency, *China: International Trade* (updated quarterly).
5. See Yitzhak Shichor, "The Middle East," in Gerald Segal and William T. Tow (editors), *Chinese Defense Policy* (Urbana and Chicago: University of Illinois Press, 1984).
6. See in particular Banning Garrett and Bonnie Glaser, *War and Peace: The Views from Moscow and Beijing* (Berkeley: University of California Press, 1984).
7. See U.S. Congress, *Allocation of Resources*, pp. 159–161.
8. *Ibid.*, pp. 162–164.
9. *Ibid.*, pp. 164–167.
10. CIA, *International Trade*.
11. U.S. Congress, *Allocation of Resources*, pp. 86, 181–182.
12. "China Belongs to the Third World Forever," *Liaowang* (Beijing), no. 5, 1981, cited in Foreign Broadcast Information Service, *Daily Report: China* (hereafter cited as FBIS/*China*), August 24, 1981, pp. A3–4.
13. Beijing Xinhua, October 19, 1981, in FBIS/*China*, October 19, 1981, pp. A1–2.
14. He Ying visited Syria and Libya in May 1982.
15. CIA, *International Trade*.

Chapter 3

DOMESTIC COMPONENTS AND CHINA'S EVOLVING THREE WORLDS THEORY

by Carol Lee Hamrin

Chinese thinking about the Third World over the decades has been closely tied with China's modern identity crisis. The question of China's role in the world since World War II, as the imperial-colonial prewar structure has been transformed into an interstate system, has been a source of psychological anxiety in the educated elite, a very practical dilemma requiring trade-offs between the goals of development and independence, and a catalyst for leadership disagreement. Mao Zedong's 1970s identification of China with the Third World in confrontation with the superpowers was the last phase in a lengthy and tortuous effort to chart a secure and independent course through the dangerous currents of the Cold War era. Too often, that independence was purchased at the price of the economy.

Birthed in international conflict and domestic controversy, Mao's combative Theory of the Differentiation of the Three Worlds has now fallen into disuse; it is being replaced gradually with concepts of peaceful cooperation. This reflects both the economic imperatives driving the Chinese leadership to accept much greater involvement with the global economy and new levels of confidence in China's ability to manage both its political and economic interests in an international environment perceived to be less hostile.

Still, this new outlook is tentative and not fully shared in the leadership. Whether it becomes more solidly established will depend on a mix of external opportunities and internal management of China's difficult transition period.

The Role of Ideology in Foreign Policy

The Three Worlds Theory, in its various guises over the years, has provided the Marxist-Leninist intellectual framework within which Chinese researchers and policymakers have viewed the international situation. The fact that the theory has been changed several times reflects changes in both the international situation and Chinese reactions to the international situation. But this is *not* to say that Three Worlds ideology has been merely ex post facto rationalization for decisions made on more practical grounds. Ideology has played a much more dynamic role, as in all political systems, whether to a greater or lesser extent. That ideology is malleable does not in any way dismiss the fact that it performs certain *functions* in shaping policy behavior.

Setting Goals

China's foreign policy has been marked consistently by efforts to create the ideal out of the real, to change the status quo into something more suited to Chinese interests. Michael Ng-Quinn has provided an analysis of the structure of the postwar international system that starkly outlines the reality of bipolarity to which a weak and poor China has been constrained to adjust.[1] But defining the logic of the system, such that China "must lean to one side," only highlights the fact that for most of the past 35 years China has sought to avoid doing just what appears so "inevitable." Defining the international constraints on Chinese action is thus only half the story; understanding the motivations and intentions behind Chinese behavior is the other. The story of Chinese foreign policy is precisely the effort to overcome the handicap of weakness based on tangible capabilities (population, military forces, technological level, and so forth) by mobilizing the intangible capabilities (such as will, diplomacy, strategy, political strength) so as to break out of the "box" of bipolarity. And Chinese Marxism has played a central role in this effort to forge an independent stance for China, particularly in defining the "enemy" and in engendering optimism that the oppressed eventually will be the victors.

Establishing Legitimacy

That policies, including foreign policies, require "justification" or "rationalization" points to something more important than cynical window dressing for naked pursuit of national interest. The most fundamental imperative for any regime, and for any individual leader, is to maintain a basic legitimacy as spokesman for the nation. In the Chinese system, this legitimacy is derived indirectly from the elite rather than from the larger populace through direct election. Ideology is a basic tool in the effort to persuade the elite of the legitimacy of a given political program. Competing programs will have competing "banners" or "campaign slogans" intended to shift the grounds of legitimacy from one set of priorities to another.

China's mid-1980s resurrection of the principles of peaceful coexistence as its guidelines in international affairs is accompanied by a prideful claim to have originated these universal principles in the mid-1950s as a unique contribution to Marxist theory. Such efforts provide China as a nation with a sense of universal mission, similar in function to Mao's more radical calls for world revolution. The authority of any leader or regime relies to some extent on providing ideological grounds for the legitimacy of the nation.

Limiting Policy Options

For any leadership anywhere, prevailing assumptions and world views, especially those shared by a whole generation of leaders, will limit the policy options that are considered in the decision process. But the enforcement of ideological orthodoxy serves even more actively to screen out ideas. For a fragmented leadership facing extremely complex choices with a minimum of expertise at head, a condition common in China's recent history, this function can have some positive short-term effects. Decisions can be made quickly within a narrow range of possibilities, and leadership unity can be preserved.

The more fundamental purpose of imposing orthodoxy, however, is to render illegitimate any policy options that would threaten the interests of those in power. The prime example here would be Maoist calls for proletarian revolution abroad to legitimate political and social discrimination against "nonproletarian" elements at home, thus retaining power. In order to legitimize new Chinese domestic policies as properly "socialist," Deng Xiaoping's reformers have dropped all accusations that the Soviet Union is *intrinsically* revisionist. The important point is that in both cases, foreign policy flexibility is constrained. In the short term, some concrete policy moves are made more difficult and others easier. In the long term, major departures in strategy required to adjust to the changing international situation are almost always postponed by the strictures against reporting, analysis, and policy recommendation that might lead to departures from established practice. Thus, major changes in policy normally occur only with a shift in the leadership and without careful forethought and planning.

These functions of ideology point to the analytical value of perusing China's evolving foreign policy line. Chinese leaders adopt given foreign policy theories to *articulate* their *perceptions* of world affairs and their *strategy* for dealing with them. In formulating both perceptions and strategy, Chinese leaders must take into account their domestic concerns as well as their international concerns. In the political process of making foreign policy decisions, a consensus must be created by balancing or trading off conflicting imperatives. Often the conflicting interests at a given time can be discerned by careful analysis of contradictions within official statements on the foreign policy "line." Changes in the domestic balance of power or a shift in leadership priorities can be illuminated by comparing changes in the line over time. Of course, a full explanation of changes in Chinese foreign policy must incorporate other lines of analysis, including an understanding of international events that force Chinese leaders to take action and constrain their options, as well as changes in the institutional structure and personalities involved in making decisions. The following discussion attempts to provide one part of the whole equation—an understanding of the evolution of the Chinese Marxist ideological framework within which foreign policy decisions have been viewed and discussed.

From Stalin's Camp to Maoist Autarky

As Mao looked out at the world in the two decades after 1949, he perceived struggle. This is not surprising considering both Mao's intellectual birth as an anti-imperialist crusader for nationalism, his decades of wartime experience as guerrilla leader, and the hostile reception of the appearance of his fledgling state on the international scene. In the fluid power situation following World War II, the Chinese found it most natural to join Stalin's effort to set up the socialist camp in competition with the capitalist-imperialist forces, then in disarray.

Marx had written about the integrated, global capitalist market that emerged with full-blown capitalism. Lenin had extrapolated from this his theory of the "era of imperialism," during which the "dying" forces of capitalism used military, economic, and cultural coercion to guarantee markets, commodities, and cheap labor in the "colonies." In the interwar period, Moscow followed Lenin's prescription that the Soviet Union and other countries on the periphery could weaken the capitalist system by breaking free politically and building up new socialist economies. After World War II Stalin branched out from Lenin's perspective to hypothesize that a new set of coordinated economic-military relationships among the newly independent countries, led by the Soviet Union, could escape the snares of the global capitalist market and overcome its weakened enemy. Although China was always uncomfortable with Soviet efforts to tightly organize the "socialist bloc," preferring a looser coalition or "united front" that would give China pride of place as an independent, influential world actor, the perception of life-or-death struggle between two implacable sets of enemies made sense in light of the Korean conflict and the U.S.-Taiwan blockade of the China coast. As late as 1957, Mao was speaking in related terms of the "east wind prevailing over the west wind."

It can be argued that Mao's militant world view, focused heavily on power politics and ignoring the realities of postwar economic trends, led to missed opportunities for China to use economic and diplomatic tools to reshape a more benign environment—first, in 1948–1949 when Truman considered adopting a neutral stance in the Chinese civil war and then during the brief post-Stalin "détente" of the mid-1950s. In both these periods, other Chinese leaders seemed to take a less suspicious view of U.S. intentions toward China and more actively pursued efforts to achieve some accommodation for economic gains. These tendencies within the leadership reflected, in part, their divergent political interests. Mao's legitimacy lay in his heroic feats as leader of the nationalist revolution, that of Zhou and others lay in nation-building.

Divergences between Soviet and Chinese perceptions, stemming from different interests, were evident early on. Stalin's "two-camp" thesis posited that U.S. intentions were to attack the Soviet Union and thus all efforts within the socialist world should focus primarily on preserving Soviet power and influence. Mao argued instead that the immediate U.S. aim was to subjugate the weak countries like China in the vast "intermediate" zone (forerunner of the Third World) between the two camps, thus building strength for an assault on its main enemy. Implicitly, of course, this called for Soviet support of anti-imperialist struggles elsewhere, especially China's. Chinese disgruntlement over Soviet reluctance to support the resumption of the Chinese Civil War in 1945–1946 for fear of sparking a U.S.-Soviet conflict was outweighed, however, by Soviet support in the Korean conflict and in China's First Five-Year Plan. In general, the Chinese were willing to follow Moscow's lead under Stalin and were relatively successful, within the two-camp framework, in using the Soviet "umbrella" to serve their interests.

After Stalin, the balance shifted, *not* least of all due to Mao's lack of respect for the post-Stalin leadership and his own pretensions as successor to Lenin and Stalin as leaders of world communism. As Khrushchev gave increasing priority to détente with the United States, Moscow proved less and less willing to support Chinese or other countries' confrontations with Washington. As the Soviet Union became an established power, fewer and fewer causes of those countries on the periphery of power and wealth were viewed as directly linked to Soviet interests. Mao's non-Stalinist geopolitical views, focused on the continuing anti-imperialist struggle in the "intermediate zone," came to the fore, as Beijing became more and more suspicious that Moscow was abandoning revolutionaries worldwide. The Great Leap Forward, in its international context, can be viewed as China's first effort to assert an independent development model and a "third" power pole, independent from the alliance systems of both Moscow and Washington. Certainly, Khrushchev perceived it as such and did his best to undermine it.

In the wake of domestic disaster, the Chinese leadership in the early 1960s was divided over how to proceed. In concert with the economic retrenchment at home, managed by Chen Yun, some international experts associated with Zhou Enlai recommended a revival of the Bandung-era principles of détente that posited accommodation through "peaceful coexistence" with the postwar status quo. This proposal to lower tensions with Moscow, initiate contacts with the West, and cease aid to revolutionaries was justified as an equivalent of Lenin's truce with capitalists at home and abroad through the new economic policies and the Treaty of Brest-Litovsk signed with Germany.

Mao and his closest supporters, Lin Biao and radical civilian leaders who had been the brain trust behind the Leap, strongly opposed this plan. To preserve their authority, they tried to limit the rollback of Leap policies and continued to raise tensions with both Moscow and Washington. Liu Shaoqi was most identified with the temporary compromise policies of the mid-1960s by which the Chinese tried to contain Sino-Soviet differences within the bounds of friendly competition, meanwhile building up the circle of Chinese clients in power in Asia and Africa so as to increase China's international leverage. By 1965, as two Chinese clients—Nkrumah in Ghana and the PKI (Indonesian Communist Party)—both ended in disaster, the United States stepped up its involvement in Indochina, and Sino-Soviet polemics strained the relationship to the limit, the stage was set for Mao's policy preferences to prevail. International trends served to shore up what had become the views of a shrinking minority in China.

Lin Biao, Mao's chosen successor, captured the essence of Mao's radical Yan'an revivalism both in his persona as war hero and in his famous 1965 speech calling for the countryside (developing world) to "encircle" the cities (developed world). For two years, China amazed the world with its efforts to launch a cultural revolution at home and foment revolutionary movements abroad to alter radically the international balance of power. During this period, both the strength of Mao's faith and the unreality of his neo-Stalinist perspective were starkly revealed. The postwar era of national revolution came to a close without in the least resembling the expected global socialist revolution. Meanwhile, China's attempts to develop in isolation were constantly disrupted by the penetration of outside events. The experiment ended abruptly in 1968, as the Chinese military leadership in Wuhan mutinied against the center and the Soviet Union invaded Czechoslovakia, making its military buildup along the Sino-Soviet border appear ominous indeed. China could no longer afford international isolation and economic and military stagnation; its very survival as a nation appeared to be threatened. With Lin Biao on the wane after 1969, the stage was set for new departures.

From Radical to Moderate Maoism

Out of the debacle emerged the more moderate anti-establishment perspective of Mao's later years, which was formalized in the Three Worlds Theory put forth by then Vice Premier Deng Xiaoping at the Sixth Special Session of the UN General Assembly in April 1974.[2] China's economic imperatives and changing international realities called for a new accommodation on its part; changes in the domestic balance of power allowed it to happen, as symbolized by the return of Deng. Chinese leaders perceived both new opportunities in the fragmenting of both "blocs," as well as dangers in continued isolation during an era of détente between the two big powers. China gradually gave up support of the few remaining Maoist splinter parties and insurrections on its borders, in the quest for improved relations with the United States and its rapidly modernizing allies all around China's periphery. Now, China sought to augment its influence by forging primary alignments with developed nations of the Second World as well as with other developing Third World nations on the common ground of political and economic nationalism rather than socialist aims.

For the first time in the mid-1970s, Mao elaborated a theory linking Moscow's "revisionist" domestic policies and "antirevolutionary" foreign policy under Khrushchev with Soviet expansionism under the Brezhnev Doctrine, which justified military intervention outside Soviet borders in order to "preserve" socialist gains (Soviet interests). Simply put, the Soviet system had become a variant of the developed West—its state monopoly of capitalism led it to pursue "social imperialism" within the Soviet bloc to guarantee its own supplies and markets for exploitation. In a sense, China was admitting that Moscow had succeeded in Stalin's aim of setting up a dual market international system; the problem was, China wanted part of neither alternative!

Chinese efforts focused on weakening the superpowers (the two sole members of the First World) by encouraging greater independence on the part of their respective European allies and supporting the demands of the Third World for a New International Economic Order. Until that goal was in sight, Beijing was constrained to tie into the existing two systems for the sake of its own economic growth. But under the rubric of "self-reliance," a high premium was placed on maintaining a self-sufficient economic and political system. Understandably, for other developing countries without the luxury of varied resources and a continental base, this new Chinese model of self-reliance held only slightly greater attraction than the radical Maoist call for complete autarky. During the 1970s, Mao's preoccupation with power politics still prevailed; little energy was devoted by China to developing creative, mutually beneficial Third World economic cooperation. In fact, Chinese economic assistance was increasingly tied to requirements of anti-Soviet behavior on the part of recipients.

A Brief "Lean to the West" and Retreat to Neutrality

During the transitional period following Mao's death, three stages can be discerned in foreign policy.[3] The first immediate tendency evident in 1977 might be termed "neo-Maoist." It retained much of Mao's highly moralistic approach to domestic and foreign policy; while China might be temporarily weak and poor, it could still be a moral exemplar in the fight against imperialism and gain international support and strength through siding with emerging historical forces. This was more than cheerleading; it tapped deep historical roots in Chinese tradition and fed on the anti-imperialist sentiments of the May 4th period. This approach reflected the desires of Hua Guofeng and his backers to inherit Maoist sources of legitimacy and forge national unity at a time of succession crisis.

Immediately upon Deng's return to power in 1977, but before he consolidated power, there was an awkward attempt at marrying residual Maoist radicalism and Deng's emerging *real politik* in a new version of the Three Worlds Theory. This restatement was published by *Renmin Ribao* in November 1977 as an authoritative article by its editorial department; actually, it was drafted under the personal direction of veteran ideologist Hu Qiaomu.[4] The intent of shoring up the authority of Maoist orthodoxy and then cloaking current policy in its folds was revealed in the title "Chairman Mao's Theory of the Differentiation of the Three Worlds Is a Major Contribution to Marxism-Leninism."

First, the article cited precedents in Lenin and Stalin for a division of the world into three main groups: the oppressed, the oppressors, and those in the middle. It then explained why the three could differ in prescribing specific alignments:

> *The transition from the capitalist to the socialist system on a global scale is a very long and tortuous process, full of complicated struggles, and it is inevitable that in the process there will be different alignments of the world's political forces in different periods.*

From there, it was a short hop to justifying cooperation with the weaker superpower, the United States, against the growing Soviet menace. For the first time, the Soviet Union was defined explicitly as the greater threat to world peace. The article also explicitly defined the socialist countries outside the Soviet bloc as members of the Third World, justifying China's new interest in expanding relations with Yugoslavia and Romania. It attacked the Gang of Four for balking at the formation of a united front that implicitly would include the United States and other nonsocialist countries, both developed and developing.

Yet, this new modification retained certain basic premises of the Maoist theoretical framework that worked to limit cooperation with the West. Both superpowers were defined as systemically imperialist:

> *The distinctive features of a superpower are as follows: Its state apparatus is controlled by monopoly capital in its most concentrated form, and it relies on its economic and military power, which is far greater than that of other countries, to carry on economic exploitation and political oppression and to strive for military control on a global scale; each superpower sets exclusive world hegemony as its goal and to this end makes frantic preparations for a new world war.*

There was explicit reference to Soviet "occupation of Chinese territory" in the north and U.S. "occupation of Taiwan" as threats to Chinese security. At the same time, the United States was depicted as still intent on making a comeback and ultimately seizing world hegemony and was therefore perceived as an ally that was "temporary, vacillating, unstable, unreliable, and conditional." Self-reliance remained the watchword.

Once Deng Xiaoping came into fuller control by the end of 1978, however, Chinese foreign policy began to reflect his preoccupation with China's modern *problematique:* how to quickly enhance the nation's wealth and power as the means to obtaining its rightful place in the world. In his view, the shortest route to success was alignment with Washington against the Soviet Union to gain a short-term "security umbrella" and long-term access to advanced technology. His interest in military cooperation served to woo the military to the reform program; his activist diplomacy enhanced his authority as China's preeminent statesman.

Reflecting Deng's interests, through the end of 1981 there was increasing talk of a global anti-Soviet united front, explicitly including the United States, China, Japan, and Europe with the Third World. Deng, alone among Chinese leaders, even spoke of long-term close cooperation with the United States. While the Three Worlds Theory became more and more rare in Chinese public discussion of foreign policy, however, a new theoretical formulation never emerged to take its place. A general ideological vacuum pervaded Chinese politics, which turned out to be the Achilles' heel of the reformers.

A third competing tendency appeared briefly in 1979, after China's ill-fated attack on Vietnam, and reemerged with a vengeance in 1981 in the general policy backlash against disruptions in China's economy and society attributable to reforms. The return to a more neutral stance toward the superpowers brought about a revival of the Three Worlds Theory, even though it now postulated correct relations rather than hostility with both big powers. The resolution on questions in party history, passed by the Sixth Plenum of the Eleventh Congress in June 1981, on the eve of the party's 60th anniversary, praised Mao for his foreign policy, including his "correct strategy of the 'three worlds' theory."[5] Not surprisingly, Hu Qiaomu, the author of the 1977 article on the theory, also drafted the historical resolution. At the Twelfth Congress in 1982, he became the Politburo member charged with overseeing ideological work in all spheres.

The new emphasis on "independence" reflected a new balance between Deng's single-minded anti-Soviet strategic focus and the economic development goals under the purview of Chen Yun and other veteran economic planners such as Li Xiannian and Bo Yibo. Their political power and authority grew at a time of economic difficulty and social disturbance, justifying a return to orthodoxy and strict central control. From their perspective, Chinese and international realities called for caution and moderation at home and abroad and, in particular, for cutbacks in the military budget. This in turn required a pullback from the provocative proto-alliance with the United States that had emerged in the wake of the Soviet invasion of Afghanistan, aversion to foreign policy adventurism, and a focus on regional rather than global matters so as to ensure a peaceful environment and congenial trade partners.

Emergence of a New "Peace" Paradigm

In 1984 the Chinese announced their support for peaceful solutions to the world's problems. In the summer, officials stressed the promotion of peace as China's major world role during the 30th anniversary celebrations of the formulation of the Bandung Era's Five Principles of Peaceful Coexistence.[6] Premier Zhao Ziyang, in a speech marking the occasion, avoided blaming the superpowers or "imperialism" alone for disrupting peace. He spoke of many differences, including those not based on class, that lead to conflict and implied that concrete efforts to strengthen cooperation were more important than blanket efforts to oppose hegemony. Zhao made no effort to give his views an orthodox cast by citing Marx, Lenin, or Mao; rather, he stressed China's contribution to the formulation of the Five Principles as international guidelines.[7]

Chinese advocacy of peace, including détente between the superpowers and an end to the arms race, has since gradually emerged as the primary theme in China's rhetoric on the global outlines of its foreign policy—becoming even more salient than other themes, including independence, antihegemony, and Third World unity. This posture as a peace activist enhances China's image at home and abroad and serves strategic interests as well. It is important, moreover, as part of a larger strategy by Deng and his successors to cement their controversial reform program in place.

The peace line has been accompanied by yet another modification of China's world view, one that points to major departures from Leninism and buries the Three Worlds Theory several feet deeper. This shift in theory buttresses iconoclastic efforts to set up a new theoretical framework for unorthodox domestic policies. This theory building, while still controversial and by no means complete, promises to provide an ideological mooring for use of capitalist elements at home and peaceful cooperation with the capitalist West *for the long term*.

Talk of Détente

Chinese pronouncements began to declare in 1984 that "the most important international issue" was to end the nuclear arms race in Europe. They were accompanied by praise for the cross-national peace movement in the West. High-ranking leaders began to assert to visitors that a general détente, including the superpowers, is a major Chinese goal. Xinhua first cited such a statement by Zhao in June 1984, when he spoke of China's desire to "defuse" world tension and of its hope for détente between East and West and between the great powers. A year later, Zhao put it this way:

> *A lasting peace, increased friendly cooperation and co-prosperity have a vital bearing on the interests of the people of all countries, and they are becoming the goal of a worldwide effort today.*[8]

This new line implies there are no *intrinsic, systemic* reasons why either superpower should post a threat to others; their pursuit of global hegemony is no longer viewed by the Chinese as inevitable. Taken together, these developments in 1984–1985 are a startling departure from the vitriolic Chinese antidétente, antisuperpower rhetoric of the 1970s and early 1980s. They accompany efforts to improve relations with both great powers for the first time since the mid-1950s.

In part, this new line serves strategic and regional interests. Calls for superpower détente fit with Chinese claims to friendly neutrality—a willingness to improve bilateral relations with each, not allying with or against either. Beyond posturing, the Chinese have spoken of their concern about a new arms race. As the Chinese continue to fall behind in relative military capability, they probably perceive a genuine interest in avoiding runaway superpower competition. Talk of a U.S.-Soviet "star wars" contest in 1984–1985, just as the Seventh Five-Year Plan was being drafted, put pressure on the Chinese from their own military to reallocate resources away from development to step up military modernization. For example, comments by an influential military veteran and adviser, former Deputy Chief of Staff Wu Xiuquan, seemed much more pessimistic about the international situation and more concerned about China's military position than most official civilian statements.[9]

The new peace line also provides a better focus for addressing regional problems. There were stepped-up efforts in the mid-1980s to resolve sources of aggravation in relations with Mongolia and Burma, as well as new initiatives regarding confederation solutions for Korea, Hong Kong, and Taiwan. Beijing's desire to diffuse regional tensions has been evident, too, in continued efforts to keep the door open for growing exchanges with Moscow, and even with Vietnam as well.

Revising Marxism

The primary immediate motive for the new peace line, however, clearly seems to be the utmost urgency for China to pursue all means to catch up with the rapid pace of development set by other Asian countries. Since 1983 the Chinese press has been filled with talk of the "new technological revolution" sweeping the world, which holds both promise and threat for China. It threatens to leave China behind in the dust if it does not adjust to reality; it promises to help China "leap" into the ranks of the development if creative use is made of a "window of opportunity" now opening.

The essence of China's emerging philosophy of international relations is its definition of a "new era" in world affairs, in which countries with "various social forms" are becoming increasingly interdependent within the context of "one world market." This theme implies a major departure from Lenin's theory of imperialism, positing a dialectical struggle between oppressors and oppressed, which was the framework for all previous Chinese "lines." Deng's "lean to the West," for example, like Mao's initial opening to the West, was premised on the expediency of aligning with a "weaker" and declining imperialist power against a greater "social imperialist" threat. Likewise, China's "independent foreign policy" line that emerged in 1982 was originally cast in Mao's Three Worlds model of contending forces. Such constructs justified U.S.-China cooperation as temporary and tactical. The new formulation, while not explicitly repudiating an eventual global Communist revolution, nevertheless posits a prolonged period of peace and cooperation rather than struggle into the indefinite future.

In a 1984 *Renmin Ribao* article, senior theorist and foreign policy adviser Huan Xiang introduced the theoretical shift.[10] He began by depicting the post–World War II era as one of struggle for independence when the Five Principles were a key *weapon* for opposing hegemony. But today, "under the current circumstances of various social forms and one world market," the Five Principles must be endowed with "new contents under the new world environment."

Huan and others have forecast a future global economy to which the economies of the socialist countries would be inextricably linked. Privately, a Chinese diplomat affirmed the new "one world market" thesis by commenting that China's adherence to Stalin's theory of "two parallel world economies" had benefited only the

Soviet Union.[11] Implicitly, this new concept repudiates former Leninist notions that capitalism is doomed, Stalin's view that a socialist bloc economy could provide protection from the vicissitudes of the capitalist market, and Maoist efforts to quarantine China through closed door "self-reliance" as well.

The development of this theory in 1984 had clear and important domestic linkages. The Chinese were aligning foreign and domestic policy trends when they stressed the need for long-term "coexistence" between capitalism and socialism at home and abroad. In preparation for the Third Plenum of the Twelfth Party Congress in fall 1984, which unveiled a bold blueprint for economic reform, the Chinese media were strongly underscoring the need for reestablishing a large private sector and maintaining a mixed economy "for a long time." The economic reform decision introduced the theoretical concept of a "socialist commodity economy."Media discussions of its meaning through 1985 openly admitted it was a new addition to Marxist theory, correcting Marx's error in pitting commodity and socialist economic forms against each other. Reformers are using this concept to reintroduce the capitalist stage of development, through which they believe China, like all countries, must pass.

It is uncertain whether the "one world market" doctrine will lead to an explicit acknowledgment in China of the end of Lenin's "age of imperialism." Some Chinese leaders and foreign affairs specialists seem reluctant to endorse the trend. The day after Zhao's July 1984 speech, conservative spokesman President Li Xiannian implicitly countered Zhao's effort to give primacy to the peace theme when he told a visitor that "the basic guideline of China's foreign policy is independence."[12] Premier Zhao's work reports to the National People's Congress annual sessions in 1984 and 1985 skirted the central issues, suggesting that a consensus view on the new line has yet to be formed.[13] Similarly, articles and speeches by Zhao and others in the spring of 1985, celebrating the 1955 Asian-African conference in Bandung, avoided theoretical issues, vaguely stringing together slogans about "national independence, world peace, friendly cooperation, and common development."[14]

Meanwhile, through 1985, international affairs specialists openly debated the theoretical issues. For example, in 1985 two researchers from the Central Party School wrote a scathing critique, "On the Contemporary Worldwide Scientific and Technological Revolution and China's Global Strategy," of a paper that had been presented at a symposium on that topic in 1984. In essence, the critique suggested that Chinese theoretical innovators were far too sanguine about the prospects for peace and cooperation. The authors underscored the continuing importance of self-reliance in the face of growing protectionism abroad, the reluctance of capitalist countries to transfer advanced technology, and the inevitability of economic crises and recessions in the capitalist world market. The critique attacked the idea that the new technical revolution would prolong the life of international capitalism by reducing its drive for domination and exploitation and improving the rationality of its organization. It imputed naive "peacenik" attitudes to those who argued that the prospects for war were diminishing. The authors concluded that

> *the establishment of worldwide economic integration is utterly impossible. . . . We must never forget that the world today is in the transition era from capitalism to socialism. . . . We hold [to] the strategic guiding ideology put forward by the CCP Central Committee and accepted by many comrades in the economic and academic circles on two kinds of resources, two markets and two types of skills. . . . [China's] economic development strategy can be correct only when it is adopted in light of this guiding ideology.*[15]

Conclusion: Domestic and International Factors in Foreign Policy

In recent years, among analysts both of Chinese foreign policy and of international relations in general, there has been a turn away from the once popular study of domestic political "decisionmaking" as a chief source of insight. Clearly disillusioned by the difficulties of understanding the complex domestic politics on many issues, including foreign policy, analysts have turned to focus on the constraints placed on Chinese decisionmakers by international "realities." Michael Ng-Quinn, for example, has offered a sound critique of the pitfalls of domestic analysis and focused instead on explaining how the bipolar nature of the postwar international structure has limited Chinese options. He reaches the rather surprising conclusion that "Chinese foreign policy has been largely consistent since the end of World War II.[16] By this, he means that China has been forced to lean toward either the United States or the Soviet Union, and all efforts to defy this systemic logic have been doomed to "inevitable" failure until China has gained enough "capability" to become a third pole and thus transform the international balance of power.

In my view, Ng-Quinn overstates the value of the following results of such analysis: Despite polemics, China's options are limited and its ability to pursue an independent posture vis-à-vis the superpowers is constrained. The *only* uncertainty is China's choice over which pole to align with and over the extent of such alignment.

The interested observer might be forgiven for asking a few more questions: *Under what circumstances* will China "lean" one way or the other? When and why would China be prompted to try a middle way, and would it be hostile or friendly to both great powers? Will China ever recognize the alleged "inevitability" of failure for such attempts and if not, why not? China's leaders might further ask: What international stance would most likely lead to strengthening China's capabilities as an independent pole? What should China do in the meantime? To bring my point home, if we apply Ng-Quinn's main thesis to the current situation and recognize that Chinese efforts to modernize rapidly while adopting a neutral but friendly stance toward the big powers are likely to be difficult, still, has not our analysis of what the Chinese will do on specific issues and, how well they will succeed, only begun?

Most observers, including Ng-Quinn, end up pointing implicitly or explicitly to analysis of Chinese politics as essential to prognosis about Chinese behavior. For example, Jonathan Pollack argues in a 1984 study that "Internal differences within the Chinese leadership were not the critical determinant in China's movement away from the United States," and yet at the same time he points to Chinese "perception" and "belief" and "efforts to establish" in his list of those factors that did determine the shift. He admits openly that Chinese *perception* of a diminished Soviet threat in recent years does not appear grounded in reality. Nowhere does he acknowledge, however, much less examine, the ways in which internal factors might have shaped such attitudinal characteristics.[17]

However difficult it may be to assess internal components, it seems impossible to avoid the conclusion that, in order to understand Chinese international behavior at any given time, one must look at both the international situation to which China must respond and the attitude toward the outside world prevailing within the Chinese leadership. The post-Mao leadership in general is characterized by a greater acceptance of the status quo in international affairs, fostered both by evidence of the persisting strength of the superpowers and the persisting weakness and division among developing nations. This greater realism reflects a profound learning experience during the Cultural Revolution that has left a distaste for radicalism.

Current previews of the next decades in the Chinese press are uniformly pessimistic that the Third World will easily overcome the debt crisis or that developed countries will give away advanced technology or easily forego using political and economic leverage to their own benefit. Nevertheless, the Chinese appear committed to persistent but moderate efforts to effect positive change over time through North-South dialogue and South-South economic and political cooperation. But China's own immediate interests will be uppermost in mind at all times; idealistic hopes of quick gain through ideological persuasion, foreign aid, or military intervention have all been dashed through the Maoist experience.

Within this general framework of thought, there are of course differences among Chinese leaders regarding specific policy options. Since 1982 there has been a move away from Deng Xiaoping's more activist involvement in international strategic affairs. This trend toward strategic neutrality in order to lower regional tensions and conserve resources, while expanding international economic relations, is likely to continue at least through the succession to Deng, as leaders focus inward on domestic matters.

Endnotes

1. Michael Ng-Quinn, "The Analytical Study of Chinese Foreign Policy," *International Studies Quarterly*, vol. 27, no. 2, June 1983, pp. 203–224.
2. Deng Xiaoping, *Speech by Chairman of the Delegation of the People's Republic of China at the Special Session of the U.N. General Assembly* (Beijing: Foreign Languages Press, 1974).
3. For a detailed discussion of the shifting balance of power among proponents of three competing domestic-foreign policy strategies in the 1976–1985 period, see Carol Lee Hamrin, "Competing 'Policy Packages' in Post-Mao China," *Asian Survey*, vol. XXIV, no. 5, May 1984, pp. 487–518.
4. Editorial Department, "Chairman Mao's Theory of the Differentiation of the Three Worlds Is a Major Contribution to Marxism-Leninism," *Renmin Ribao*, October 31, 1977, in Foreign Broadcast Information Service, *Daily Report:*

People's Republic of China (hereafter cited as FBIS/*China*), November 1, 1977, pp. A1–37. A Chinese foreign affairs official, who told me the identity of the author, remarked that at the time he and his colleagues thought the article was "pure sh--."

5. "Resolution on Certain Questions in the History of Our Party Since the Founding of the People's Republic of China (adopted by the Sixth Plenary Session of the Eleventh Central Committee of the Communist Party of China on June 27, 1981)," *Hongqi* (Beijing), no. 13, July 1, 1981, pp. 3–27.

6. These principles were first incorporated in agreements between China and Burma and China and India in 1954, which touched on border disputes, and then were included in the formal statements at the Afro-Asian Conference in Bandung, Indonesia, the next year. Zhou Enlai was the central Chinese actor in these events.

7. Beijing Xinhua, July 18, 1984, in FBIS/*China*, July 18, 1984, pp. A1–2.

8. Zhao Ziyang in remarks to the British Royal Institute of International Affairs as quoted by Xinhua, June 6, 1985, in FBIS/*China*, June 6, 1985, p. G4.

9. Wu Xiuquan in comments inaugurating a special page, "International Military Affairs," in *Jiefangjun Bao*, September 23, 1985, cited the same day by Zhongguo Xinwen She, in FBIS/*China*, September 24, 1985, p. K22. Wu spoke of "the danger of war and the expansion of war just below the surface" and the "escalation of threats to peace."

10. Huan Xiang, "The Five Principles of Peaceful Coexistence Are Principles for World Peace and Development," *Renmin Ribao*, July 18, 1984, p. 6, in FBIS/*China*, July 18, 1984, pp. A3–6.

11. Personal conversation.

12. Beijing Xinhua, July 18, 1984, in FBIS/*China*, July 19, 1984, p. I1.

13. Zhao Ziyang, "Report on the Work of the Government," May 15, 1984, in FBIS/*China*, June 1, 1984, pp. K1–20, and same title, March 27, 1985, in FBIS/*China*, March 27, 1985, pp. K5–7.

14. See Beijing Xinhua, April 24, 1985, in FBIS/China, April 25, 1985, pp. A3–5; and Li Shenzhi, *Renmin Ribao*, April 19, 1985, p. 7.

15. Wu Jian and Weng Zhixing, "Understanding of a Few Points on Development—A Discussion with Comrades Zhu Jiaming and Huang Jiangnan," *Shijie Jingji* (Beijing), no. 6, June 10, 1985, pp. 45–52, in U.S. Joint Publications Research Service, *Chinese Economic Affairs* (JPRS-CEA-85-078), August 28, 1985, pp. 1–12.

16. Ng-Quinn, "Analytical Study."

17. Jonathan D. Pollack, summary to *The Lessons of Coalition Politics: Sino-American Security Relations* (Santa Monica, CA: RAND Report R-3133-AF, May 1984), pp. v–vi; and "China and the Global Strategic Balance," in Harry Harding (editor), *China's Foreign Relations in the 1980s* (New Haven: Yale University Press, 1984), p. 164.

Chapter 4

CHINA'S THIRD WORLD POLICY AS A COUNTERPOINT TO THE FIRST AND SECOND WORLDS

by Sarah-Ann Smith

Since coming to power, and in the Yan'an days before that, China's Communist leadership has used its Third World policy as a means of defining the Chinese self-image. Thus China has been consistently defined as peaceful, unified with the developing nations— the "underdogs"—as not hegemonic and not a superpower. Through this conceptualization China seeks to contrast itself with what it describes as the moribund superpowers, to exemplify its claim to being a "new thing" on the world scene.

This self-definition has never hindered China from pursuing goals of national self-interest vis-à-vis either of the superpowers or within the regions of most concern to it, that is, those areas contiguous to Chinese soil. In terms both of security and China's attaining a world role commensurate with its self-definition, relations with the two superpowers are and always have been central on the level of pragmatic foreign policy. However, this does not negate the importance of China's policy toward the Third World. If anything, it makes it even more significant, as a means of indicating the limits to which China may be willing to go in relations with either superpower and by exemplifying China's continued resistance to accepting superpower assumptions as the basis for the conduct of its own foreign relations. On a practical level, China has in most cases carried out its relations with Third World countries in a manner unlike that of either the United States or the Soviet Union. In addition, China's image of itself has led its leaders to take independent policy positions, and, at this point in its history, to eschew formal alliance with both the United States and the Soviet Union.

Two questions are raised when one begins to examine China's Third World policy in light of the above: Is China's current policy toward developing countries consistent with its past practice? In light of the importance of the two superpowers to China's foreign policy goals, does its Third World policy matter?

Historical Development of China's "Counterpoint" Approach

The basis of China's definition of itself in relation to the Third World was expounded at least as early as 1936 in Mao Zedong's conversation with Edgar Snow. Mao described China as a model which would set the example, spur the cause of revolution, and provide the pattern of development in all colonial areas. Not only was China the harbinger of a new, liberated world, but China's development experience would draw all to it by its excellence.[1]

The Traditional World View

In a certain sense this idea is continuous with the traditional Confucian world view. Two assumptions characterized that traditional world view: the hierarchical nature of relationships and the idea of Chinese cultural superiority. It projected an emperor reaching out and drawing all into the Chinese sphere by the example of his virtue. It can be argued that the pattern of the relationship between the domestic and external orders has continued, though the content has changed. Thus the Chinese image of itself as a model of revolution that would draw all to it by its excellence finds its parallel in the traditional image of the world as an extension of the Confucian order.

Approaches Vis-à-Vis the Soviet Union

Since 1949 China has used its Third World theories in several ways as it has related to the superpowers. These theories have provided the conceptual tools for China to develop its policy toward areas and issues of the Third World. Policy includes rhetoric, and China's concept of the Third World has provided the basis for its commentary on events when media coverage is the main or only course of action taken, as it often is. The component of antihegemony has provided the rationale for Chinese criticism of superpower policies—both those of the United States and those of the Soviet Union. Most important, China has used its own approach to the Third World to distance itself from superpower policies repugnant to it or considered to be counterproductive.

China's approach to the Third World has gone through numerous stages, as indicated in Carol Hamrin's chapter. These stages in part reflect its evolving self-concept vis-à-vis the superpowers. Thus the doctrine of "leaning to one side," while demanded by the political necessities of the moment and perhaps precipitated by U.S. refusal to deal with the newly founded People's Republic, was also rooted in Mao's understanding of the role of the Soviet Union. Mao had concluded that for the colonies there could be no intermediate position between the socialist Soviet Union and the capitalist nations, since the oppressor of the colonies was imperialism.[2] His goal at that time was to conquer the imperialists, and he was not yet counting the Soviet Union as one of those. Hence the close alliance with the existing socialist state—the Soviet Union.

However, political realities, and the ages-long conflict with the Soviet Union, intervened in these idealistic formulations, and the honeymoon era with the Soviet Union was short-lived. One might speculate that even in the early 1950s the Chinese were uncomfortable with the results of the Soviet approach in the developing world itself. Still committed to their own revolutionary rhetoric, they were beginning to perceive that they were in fact in competition with the Soviets among the Third World nations, and not always winning. Given their own fear of Soviet power, they could not have been sanguine about the extension of Moscow's power in the Third World. The culmination of their anxiety may be seen in the next decade when they withdrew from, or were forced out, of a number of Third World activities rather than participate when other nations refused to ostracize the Soviets.

The Five Principles of Peaceful Coexistence early on became the means of relating to countries with differing political systems. At the same time, though, China continued to view itself as a model for the developing nations to follow, both in terms of the pattern of its revolution and of its subsequent socialist development. Although Zhou Enlai found it necessary to defend China against the allegations of subversion of Third World governments at the Bandung Conference in 1955, the Chinese leadership for the most part failed to perceive the basic contradiction between an approach based on the Five Principles and setting itself up as a model for revolution. In the ensuing years it emphasized first one and then the other aspect, or both at the same time, depending on the vicissitudes of its ideological approach. Its most radical phases coincided with the period during which it was breaking with the Soviet Union, when it was immersed in ideological justification of that event, and with the early years of the Cultural Revolution. At that time, looking north to the Soviet Union and south to U.S. involvement in Vietnam, China perceived itself as surrounded by two hostile superpowers. Its conceptual approach to the outside world was thus rather naturally characterized by Lin Biao's 1965 essay "Long Live the Victory of People's War."

Rapprochement with the United States

During the first 20 years of its existence the People's Republic saw little to give it hope of improving relations with the United States. The intermittent talks in Geneva and later in Warsaw accomplished little, and the great wedge driven between the two nations by the Korean War was kept in place by U.S. policies toward Indochina, the resulting development of SEATO, what China perceived as the neocolonialist U.S. approach to the Third World generally, and harsh U.S. anti-Communist rhetoric. Therefore, this half of its superpower relations remained static during the People's Republic's first two decades, while the vicissitudes with the Soviet Union required much change in both doctrine and policy.

Parallel Development

On a practical level, China's relationships developed on two parallel lines, one through its ties with established governments and the other through contacts with and aid to national liberation movements. Though limited by its own meager resources, China engaged in a number of carefully selected aid projects, which demonstrated its commitment to a nonimperialist style of self-help, most dramatically exemplified by the TanZam Railway project. These and its active involvement in the Non-Aligned Movement and other Third World conference-type activities were designed to demonstrate its own anti-imperialist approach to aid and to identify it with those nations that continued to suffer the effects of colonialism. However, as noted above, the complications surrounding continued Soviet involvement in the conferences led China to move more into unilateral activities by the mid-1960s. Beijing's ties with and aid to national liberation movements may have been motivated in part by rivalry with the Soviet Union. It also reflected the primary goal of ridding these countries of what China viewed as reactionary capitalist regimes and, in many cases, excessive U.S. influence.

Sino-Soviet rivalry as well as the anti-U.S. stance also motivated Chinese support of North Vietnam. As became apparent, this support was never free of complications, and the Vietnamese leadership suppressed its own internal disagreements over relations with its two benefactors in order not to jeopardize much needed aid from either.

The changes toward more openness and the increasing emphasis on normal diplomatic ties which characterized Chinese conceptualizations and policy in the 1970s were strongly influenced both by the changing U.S. role in Asia and by the changing U.S. position on China itself. The effects of these policy shifts were demonstrated not only by the Chinese themselves, but also by other countries. Thus, both Beijing's accession to the UN seat in 1971 and the beginning of the process of normalizing relations with the United States enhanced the legitimacy of the People's Republic in the eyes of the rest of the world and opened the floodgates of diplomatic recognition, with country after country changing its representation from Taipei to Beijing. China was now in a position to play an active role in international conferences. It involved itself particularly in those focusing on the unique difficulties of Third World nations, once more demonstrating its avowed solidarity with the Third World and setting itself apart from either superpower.

The overthrow of the Gang of Four in 1976 made it possible for China to pursue with vigor the moderate, open approach to foreign policy that had been begun. Beijing continued to have as one of its goals the restoration of diplomatic relations with the United States. At the same time Mao's Three Worlds Theory, positing a worldwide united front against both superpowers, became the dominant conceptual expression of Chinese foreign policy. This theory represented an ideological commitment in the immediate aftermath of the death of Mao to continue and develop the Marxist-Leninist line. On a more practical level, it provided the Chinese with a set of concepts by which they could pursue their moderate foreign policy while maintaining a discreet distance from both superpowers and waiting to see what would happen with the United States.

The Post-Mao Period

Importantly, during this immediate post-Mao period, the Chinese were attempting to resolve some of the conflict between support of revolution and relations with countries having differing social systems. CCP Chairman Hua Guofeng, in his report to the Eleventh Party Congress in 1977, stated that since revolution cannot be exported, it is up to the true Marxist-Leninists in each country to combine the Communist doctrine with the particular conditions prevailing in their own country and lead the revolution to victory.[3] This may have been an attempt at indirect reassurance to legitimate governments that they had nothing to fear from China.

As for the superpowers, throughout the 1970s the Chinese defined the Soviet Union as the principle enemy, characterized as more dangerous than the other imperialist enemy, the United States.[4] Slowly the Chinese leadership was trying to develop a policy toward the Third World that was both different from and competitive with the Soviet approach. While continuing its adamant rhetorical position against Soviet imperialism, Beijing was refining its own tendency to require Third World nations to take sides, as it had done in the mid-1960s. The entire effort was hampered by lack of Chinese resources for aid and a general lack of aggressiveness toward and knowledge of parts of the world remote from its own borders.

In sum, the 1970s Third World policy was characterized by a euphoric Chinese response to renewed diplomatic ties. Hence, the mushrooming of official visits. More importantly, in typical fashion, in the Three Worlds Theory, the Chinese were using the

Third World as a means of expressing their current attitude toward the superpowers.

Premises for a "Counterpoint" Approach in the 1980s

Chinese foreign policy changes in the 1980s have been as radical as the changes in domestic policy. By the early part of the decade China had downplayed its theme of being a model for the developing nations, as well as ceasing to use rhetoric which might activate fears that it was aiding Communist insurgent organizations, particularly in Southeast Asia, its primary area of interest. China has shifted its emphasis back to the Five Principles as a framework for relationships among equals and has stressed the idea that China is part of the Third World, a developing nation among developing nations. It also maintains the importance of Third World nations joining together to solve the problems they are mutually facing. Concomitant with this emphasis, the Chinese have moved away from the three worlds approach to an independent foreign policy which seeks to distance China's policies from those of either the United States or the Soviet Union while maintaining a position from which to relate independently to both superpowers. The elements of this approach are contained in Hu Yaobang's address to the Twelfth National Party Congress in September 1982:

> *The successes China has achieved in its revolution and construction provide a powerful support to the world's movement for progress and a bright future, and conversely, our successes would have been impossible without the struggles of the people of other countries for a bright future. China has received help from other countries and peoples, and in turn has helped others. . . . Our adherence to an independent foreign policy accords with the discharging of our lofty international duty to safeguard world peace and promote human progress. . . . China never attaches itself to any big power or group of powers and never yields to pressure from any big power. . . . Revolution cannot be exported but can occur only by the choice of the people of the country concerned. It is on the basis of this understanding that we have always abided by the five principles of peaceful coexistence. . . . China and many other developing countries in Asia, Africa and Latin America sympathize with and support one another, and have enhanced their cooperation in all fields. . . . Socialist China belongs to the Third World. China has experienced the same sufferings as most other Third World coun-*

tries, and she is faced with similar problems and tasks. . . . China is
still a developing country, but we have always done our best to help
other Third World countries.[5]

National People's Congress Chairman Peng Zhen expressed the
same ideas in his elaboration of the new state constitution in
December of the same year. Noting that the constitution contained
China's commitment to an independent foreign policy and to the
Five Principles, Peng said, "We will . . . persist in treating all
countries, big or small, as equals and consistently stand on the side
of all oppressed nations and developing countries as well as other
countries and people working for world peace."[6] Statements by
various leaders and authoritative publications since then have
reiterated these positions.

In his report to the National People's Congress Session in May
1984, Premier Zhao Ziyang drew out three aspects of China's
foreign policy as being most significant. They were safeguarding
world peace, upholding the Five Principles, and strengthening
unity and cooperation with other Third World countries. Zhao also
stressed a theme the Chinese have occasionally highlighted since
the mid-1970s: China's support for the establishment of a new
international economic order.[7] A *Liaowang* article in early 1985
predicted that in 1985 China would expand its economic relations
with Third World countries more rapidly than previously. The
article cited comments by Deng Xiaoping that South-South cooperation is one of the most important aspects of China's policy of
opening up to the outside world. Deng said that those who thought
this opening was only to the developed world were mistaken.[8]

Interrelating Concepts

China's current conceptual emphases concerning the Third World
are part of its "independent foreign policy," which began to be
apparent in mid-1981. This was explained by foreign affairs specialist Wang Bingnan in a January 1983 radio broadcast. Wang noted
two distinguishing features of the independent foreign policy:
First, China does "not dance to any other country's tune"; second,
this foreign policy is determined by a long-range strategy and is
not influenced by expediency or by the provocation or instigation
of others. Wang cited the three aspects described above, stating
that safeguarding world peace involved opposing hegemonic practices and rivalry in the Third World, which is, he said, the primary
source of world tension.[9]

The interrelationship of these concepts demonstrates the typical way China continues to use its stance toward the Third World to define the pattern of its relationship to the two superpowers and as a means of maintaining its distance from them. Chinese explanations of their policy are, of course, idealized if not self-serving. While the independent foreign policy is no doubt conceived as a long-range strategy, it is also subject to change based on changing relationships with the superpowers and on international developments in general. Any particular Chinese policy approach represents a conceptualized reaction to very real events and to perceptions of Chinese self-interest. The Third World element of Beijing's 1980's policy is indeed expedient, as China's Third World policy has been in the past. The purpose of the independent foreign policy is to position the Chinese so that they can ease into a more amicable relationship with the Soviet Union while continuing to develop ties with the United States. At the same time, it enables them to preserve the option of differing with either or both superpowers on certain Third World issues.

"China Is Partial to Neither Side"

Shijie Zhishi's year-ender for 1983 (published as its "New Year Chat on the International Situation in 1984") was more explicit. The article stated that China's image of being independent became more apparent during 1983. Furthermore, of China's position vis-à-vis the contention between the superpowers, it said, "China is partial to neither side."[10] A *Guoji Wenti Yanjiu* article analyzing the events of 1983 was unusually harsh toward the United States, asserting that it "is decaying step by step" and that greater difficulties would ensue if it continued to extend its lines in pursuit of contention with the Soviet Union. The article judged that the relative strength of the two sides is balanced. Further, it said, the ability of both to influence the international situation is diminishing, due to the Third World trend to solve its own problems and oppose interference by the superpowers.[11]

Thus Beijing has ostensibly moved from the position of the late 1970s when it was tilting slightly toward the United States to the more equidistant stance of the "independent foreign policy," with its emphasis on the Third World the means by which it demonstrates this independence. Except for one important element—the partial rapprochement with the Soviet Union—the change is more theoretical than actual. The Chinese continue to rely heavily on the United States for economic exchange and technological know-how, as well as to provide a strategic balance against the Soviet Union.

The Chinese have apparently adopted their current stance based in part on an assessment that the two superpowers are, as one 1985 analysis put it, "roughly balanced" militarily.[12] As a result, Beijing made the decision to mend some of its fences with the Soviet Union in an attempt to ease the threat on its borders. This does not lessen the importance it attaches to continued U.S. opposition to Soviet policy in general and in Afghanistan and Southeast Asia particularly. At the same time the Chinese leadership remains convinced that the Third World is a major component in any long-term projection of the course of international politics. It may well have made the judgment that it was necessary to distance China from U.S. policies on certain Third World issues and areas, such as Central America. The Chinese continue to see the Third World as a major part of their own sphere of influence, and they do not want to jeopardize their relationship with it. This is important to them both because they envision themselves as a leader of the Third World and because they fear Third World development as a threat to their own international role.

A September 1984 *Renmin Ribao* article, examining China's solidarity with the Third World, added a new point to the current position. It noted that some Third World nations, due to their judgment of their own needs and situation, receive support from one or the other superpower. The article declared that China will neither condemn them for this, nor interfere. It added that since different histories have led to different choices of social systems and policies, no one should meddle. But all are opposed to imperialism, colonialism, and hegemony, and all are seeking development. It is in these goals that one finds the basis of the unity of the Third World, to which China continues to lend its support and with which it identifies.[13] This adds a subtle new element to China's current independent foreign policy, distancing it still further from what it perceives as the hegemonic involvement of both the United States and the Soviet Union in the Third World, while exonerating Third World nations which choose to accept superpower aid. It also puts the Chinese in a more tenable position from which to relate to the Third World, preserving their ideological point of view while carrying the permissiveness of the Five Principles much further than they have previously done.

Pursuing a "Counterpoint" Approach in the 1980s

An examination of specific Chinese policies toward several Third World issues will demonstrate the uses of the conceptual position described above. Consideration of Chinese activities and commentary in relation to these issues exemplifies the varying ways China pursues its policy goals and sets itself apart from the United States and the Soviet Union, while aligning itself with one or the other as expediency or its own policy preference requires.

Counter to Soviet Involvement in Asia

In its general stance, Beijing makes it quite clear that it does not want to be identified with the policies of either superpower in the Third World. It remains strongly opposed to the Soviet Union's presence in Afghanistan and Vietnam. The latter issue has led the Chinese into a very active Southeast Asia policy designed to counter the continuing Soviet alliance with Hanoi. Beijing has been moved by the former to make a number of tentative moves toward rapprochement with India, while carefully maintaining its long-standing and essential relationship with Pakistan.

When speculation of a deeper Sino-Soviet rapprochement emerged, as occurred when Mikhail Gorbachev succeeded Valentin Chernenko, Beijing was quick to remind everyone, the United States and the Soviet Union included, that still standing were the three conditions for normalization (Soviet withdrawal from Afghanistan, cessation of support to Vietnam's Kampuchea policy, and pullback from the military buildup on China's northern border).[14] Moreover, in the early-1980s the Chinese have not found themselves in agreement with the Soviets on any specific Third World issue. By contrast, they are able to cooperate with the United States quite handily in Southeast Asia, a circumstance that may belie their protestations of equidistance.

U.S. Economic Hegemony

Compared with its media treatment of the Soviet Union, China's public criticisms of the United States range over a broader spectrum of issues and areas, and negative media comments are more frequent. A February 1985 *Shijie Zhishi* article examining U.S. foreign policy in general charged that the United States, in its overemphasis on the Soviet Union's culpability for turmoil in the Third World, demands that developing countries subordinate their own interests and strategic needs to those of the United States. It also predicted that the United States will continue to practice economic hegemony and oppose the efforts of Third World countries to establish a new international economic order.[15]

Such an indictment, of course, ignores China's own penchant for condemning Soviet activities in the Third World. It also conveniently overlooks the deepening Chinese economic relationship with the United States. Must one conclude then that the Chinese do not believe their own rhetoric? More likely, they are in a credibility warp between their own actions and what they judge to be right for the rest of the world. Thus they look at superpower political and economic policies and see clearly how they lead to domination and exploitation. At the same time, exercising the age-old Chinese capacity for overlooking its own faults, Beijing sees no reason to examine its own actions in light of these criticisms.

Opposition to Superpower Third World Policies

Toward both the United States and the Soviet Union, China has developed several themes of disagreement, which remain relatively consistent. These include opposition to the policies of both in southern Africa, Central America, and the Middle East, as well as the basic concerns over Soviet policy cited previously. It said relatively little in the early 1980s about southern Africa. China maintains its own relationship to the black African nations through a stream of visits back and forth, particularly with those countries with which it has achieved close relations over the years. In 1985, for instance, Tanzanian President Julius Nyerere paid a state visit to China, as did a Tanzanian military delegation. A Chinese delegation traveled to Mozambique to take part in the celebrations marking the tenth anniversary of the independence of that country. Zimbabwean leader Robert Mugabe visited China, and a protocol expanding Chinese economic assistance and bilateral trade relations was signed with Nigeria.

As the situation in South Africa, and concomitant demonstrations in the United States, grew more volatile and dramatic in 1985, the Chinese press carried several commentaries criticizing U.S. policies and contrasting its own position. An August *Renmin Ribao* article scored the United States for abstaining on a UN

Security Council resolution condemning apartheid, saying that U.S. abstention had led South African authorities to intensify their suppressive actions against blacks. The article contrasted the administration's position of what it called "constructive contact" with the U.S. congressional resolution calling for sanctions, which it described as conforming to the trend of the times and thus furthering U.S. national interests. A Xinhua commentary during the same period emphasized the view that U.S. policy encouraged Pretoria to intensify its pursuit of apartheid policies. While acknowledging indications of some changes in U.S. policy, it was pessimistic about any dramatic turnaround. Another Xinhua commentary elaborated the Chinese point of view that suppression of black resistance in South Africa would only lead to intensified opposition. Tracing developments in 1984 and 1985 to demonstrate that this was happening, it said the struggle of blacks was gaining momentum and would not end until they achieved political rights.[16]

These comments and activities are typical of current Chinese policy toward Africa. Beijing clearly sees South Africa as the most crucial African problem at present. However, the comparatively scant attention given the issue suggests that it is not high on the Chinese agenda. While the Chinese feel compelled from time to time to score the United States on this subject, they have apparently judged that the situation is not crucial in terms of superpower rivalry and that other problems, particularly in the Middle East and Central America, provide more useful opportunities to criticize the United States.

In fact, the Chinese currently consider the Middle East and Central America to be flashpoints of superpower rivalry. In relation to both areas, Beijing has been far more vocal in its criticism of U.S. than of Soviet policy. The Chinese regularly contrast their own approach to these areas with that of the two superpowers.

U.S. Support to Israel

Some of China's most biting criticism of U.S. policies has focused on U.S. support of Israel. Beijing's opposition has long stemmed from a judgment that U.S. policies are counterproductive and thus provide an opening for the expansion of Soviet influence. For instance, a fall 1984 commentary charged that the "muddled" U.S. policy in the Middle East has encouraged the Soviets to reenter the region. About the same time the U.S. veto of a Security Council resolution on the Lebanon crisis led *Renmin Ribao* to comment that the veto demonstrated anew U.S. "support for Israeli aggression and expansion and its hostility toward the Lebanese and Arab peoples." The article warned, "Those who support aggressors will fare no better than the aggressors themselves." A March 1985 domestic radio broadcast branded the United States and Israel as the main obstacles to peace in the Middle East.[17]

China's own approach to the Middle East is described in a 1984 *Shijie Zhishi* interview with foreign policy adviser He Ying. He characterized China as the Arab world's most reliable friend and pledged continued Chinese support for the Arabs and continued refusal to interfere, contrasting this position with that of the United States. He also said the dominant issue in the region is the conflict between the Arabs and Israel, backed by the United States. The key to a solution, he said, is to resolve the Palestine problem. He predicted that the United States will have to pay for its pro-Israel policy in the area.[18]

American Involvement in Central America

Although traditionally Latin America has been at the periphery of China's foreign policy interests, the Chinese leadership also has taken a strong stand against U.S. anti-Sandinista activities, which it considers shortsighted and a violation of Nicaragua's sovereignty. Several 1984 *Renmin Ribao* commentaries condemned the U.S. mining of Nicaraguan ports and criticized the U.S. firing on "Nicaraguan merchant vessels," one saying that the latter act heightens tension in the area. The mining was viewed by this commentary as a demonstration that the United States was moving closer and closer to intervention in Central America. It supported the Contadora Group position—which is also the Chinese position—that Central American affairs should be settled through peaceful negotiations by the Central American people themselves.[19]

A September 1984 article noted that, though the United States claims that its policies of increasing military aid and installations are working, even friends of the United States in the area, such as Honduras and the Salvadoran leadership, are uneasy. They fear that the U.S. military buildup will destabilize, rather than help, and may heighten the danger instead of increasing security.[20] The

1984 *Renmin Ribao* year-ender on Central America reiterated these themes while noting fragile signs of hope in the activities of the Contadora Group and in discussions between the United States and Nicaragua, the United States and Cuba, and between government and guerrilla leaders in El Salvador.[21] For its part, demonstrating its position that Latin American problems should be resolved by the people of the region themselves, China has supported the Contadora Group's recommendations on Central America.

A *Shijie Zhishi* analysis examined in detail the 200 years of U.S. policy toward Latin America and contained particularly sharp criticism of U.S. involvement in the region. It charged that the United States has always treated Latin America as a "strategic region in its drive for world hegemony," using many methods over the years to pursue its goals. These have included propping up proxies, engineering coups, and plundering and controlling local economies through aid and loans. All these have failed, the article concluded. Looking at the Latin American policies of recent U.S. administrations, it judged that Ronald Reagan's policy is tougher than that of his predecessors and reflects "the essence of U.S. hegemony." While it may succeed for a time, its ultimate failure is inevitable.[22] This assessment was reiterated in exceedingly strong, even condemnatory language in several commentaries following President Reagan's call for "removal" of the Sandinista government during a February 1985 press conference.[23]

Countering Hegemony in Southeast Asia

Southeast Asia is by far the most important Third World area to China, and the amount of activity and attention shown it bears this out. It is a *primary arena* of Chinese foreign policy initiative and represents China's most active attempt to carry out its stated goals—to counter Soviet hegemony, develop and enhance its cooperation with the United States, and carve out a pattern of relationships independent from either superpower. It may also exemplify the pursuit of an unstated goal: to reassert regional leadership that the Chinese lost in the modern era and failed to regain through support of Vietnam in more recent decades.

In many ways Southeast Asia exemplifies the failure of Chinese policies of the 1960s and the early 1970s, which focused on support for North Vietnam and the Communist insurgencies in Indochina and throughout the region. At the same time it demonstrates the Chinese ability to do a policy aboutface and make a major attempt to recoup its losses. This attempt has been only partially successful, and Beijing's forceful pursuit of its goal of isolating Hanoi has had the effect of pushing the Vietnamese leadership into closer alliance with the Soviet Union.

The breakup of the alliance with Hanoi and the increasing Vietnamese involvement with the Soviet Union have forced the Chinese into a major effort to develop amicable relations with the ASEAN nations. This was, and remains, an exceedingly difficult task, hampered by regional suspicions and fears of Chinese intentions. It seems that at least two things are necessary: China must make its role in the settlement of the Kampuchean question a major one, while bringing the ASEAN position on this matter closer to its own, and Beijing must demonstrate its good faith to the ASEAN nations by backing off from its traditional support of Communist insurgent organizations in the region. The Chinese leadership has not yet been sufficiently sensitive to a third source of deep-seated suspicion, that surrounding its attitude toward the resident overseas Chinese population of Southeast Asia.

One of China's continuing difficulties is the divergent perception of the danger of Soviet activities in the area. The ASEAN nations are not entirely convinced that either Vietnam or the Soviet Union is a greater threat than China. Malaysia, moreover, is not yet convinced that Chinese support of the outlawed Malaysian Communist party and guerrilla organization has ceased.

In spite of these difficulties, China has so far succeeded in its major goal, that of assuming a significant role in efforts to reach an acceptable settlement in Kampuchea. It has achieved this by modifying its own position from time to time, as it has observed the limits to its ability to impose its will on the ASEAN group, and by playing to ASEAN's commitment to unity, in order to accomplish the minimum Chinese requirement—that the Khmer Communist group be included in the coalition opposing the Heng Samrin regime. It has also undertaken bilateral efforts with the United States, both to influence Washington's policy and ensure that we do not negotiate with the Vietnamese and to obtain support for its preferred position. However, in keeping with its position that regional problems should be solved by the countries in the region, its major activities have been with the ASEAN nations themselves.

China pursues its Southeast Asia policy by a *variety of means*, consulting with ASEAN, primarily through the Thai, on developments in Kampuchea, and keeping the rhetorical heat on the Vietnamese by regular verbal blasts charging them with covering up their "expansionist designs" with insincere peace proposals. In addition, there are a number of visitors back and forth, mostly to China, ranging from high-level government officials to friendship groups and cultural and economic delegations. A breakthrough of sorts occurred in 1985, when Foreign Minister Wu Xueqian was invited by Indonesia to attend the 30th anniversary meeting commemorating the Bandung Conference. Indonesia also reestablished trade relations with China in 1985.

Neutralizing Superpower Influence

China is much less actively involved in other parts of the world, depending far more on media comment to pursue its goals. While its anti-Soviet position remains strong, Beijing is less able to support U.S. Third World policies in general—and has been less able to influence those policies. Its opposition to the U.S. approach in many parts of the Third World apparently stems from the Chinese judgment that U.S. policies will not succeed either in neutralizing Soviet influence or in terms of bilateral relations with the countries themselves.

The Middle East. In the Middle East, for instance, the hallmark of China's own policy for years has been strong support for the Arab position, including support for the PLO and Yasir Arafat. The Chinese point of view reflects an assessment of the long-term necessity of responding adequately to the demands of Palestinian nationalism. While Chinese support of the Palestinian cause has been constant, Beijing has radically altered its position of supporting armed revolution, a change in keeping with its current commitment to moderation in both domestic and foreign affairs. In this connection, the Chinese preference for Arafat, the head of Fatah and the chief representative of the moderate Palestinian faction, has become even more important in recent years despite Arafat's decline in authority.

With the exception of its regular contacts with and support for Fatah and a variety of other Palestinian organizations, China's relationship with the Middle East has been pursued primarily through comments on events and on the actions of various participants. To a lesser extent it is carried out through trade and small amounts of aid. Chinese criticism of U.S. policy has been a major mode of expressing Beijing's own position, which includes a strong anti-Israel stance and of course a desire to minimize Soviet involvement in the region.

Southwest Asia. Chinese concern about superpower hegemony and its long-term effects both on the victim countries and the expansion of superpower control is demonstrated by its position on the Iran-Iraq war. Chinese commentary on this conflict usually states Beijing's anxiety that the war will lead to superpower intervention. Media coverage of the spring 1985 bombing of civilian targets on both sides emphasized the danger of superpower intervention and observed that continuation of the "meaningless" war provided exactly what the two superpowers want: a weakening of the two sides, which paves the way for intervention.[24] At the same time, China has not been beyond exploiting the conflict for its own purposes, selling arms to both sides as part of its deepening involvement in international arms trade for purely monetary gain.

South Asia. Given Chinese anxiety about the Soviet presence in Afghanistan, one might expect an active policy toward the South Asian subcontinent similar to Chinese efforts in Southeast Asia. Beijing would no doubt like to undermine the Soviet-Indian relationship while maintaining close ties with Pakistan. However, past Sino-Indian and Indian-Pakistani problems have compelled the Chinese leadership to tread gingerly. China encourages Indian-Pakistani rapprochement by praising bilateral efforts and perhaps also by privately urging the Pakistanis in this direction. The Chinese also take advantage of opportunities to further Sino-Indian relations. In the spring of 1985 the Chinese held celebrations in Beijing and at their embassy in New Delhi commemorating the 35th anniversary of the establishment of diplomatic relations.

Beijing seeks a delicate balance in encouraging India to distance itself from the Soviets. Apparently the Chinese have decided a blunt critical approach would be counterproductive. Hence, a commentary following Rajiv Gandhi's 1985 visit to Moscow described India's closeness to the Soviet Union in mild terms while highlighting the divergence of views on the all-important Afghanistan issue and on Moscow's continuing effort to develop a Soviet-dominated pan-Asian peace and security zone. The commentary praised Gandhi's effort to pursue a more amicable relationship with the United States and also noted his interest in furthering Sino-Indian relations.[25]

The Chinese cannot afford to jeopardize their relations with Pakistan in order to improve ties with India. It is partly for this reason that they have encouraged Indian-Pakistani rapproachement. Beijing continues its own close ties with the Pakistanis, a large element of which consists of the exchange of military technology. Exemplifying this military connection, Chinese Defense Minister Zhang Aiping visited Pakistan in the summer of 1985.

All these efforts are designed to further China's goal of securing its northwestern frontier and specifically to counter any Soviet attempt at further expansion from its foothold in Afghanistan. The Chinese use their Third World, antisuperpower policy as a means to achieve this goal, challenging both Indians and Pakistanis to resist hegemony. Beneath their public position, they play a complicated game of power balancing, seeking to change the configuration of alliances and antagonisms in the subcontinent to one more favorable to their purposes.

Southeast Asia. This analysis of some of China's current policies demonstrates Beijing's flexibility in utilizing a number of approaches as the situation requires and as Chinese capability allows. In general, China uses a combination of visits, media attention and commentary, and involvement in specific negotiation-type activities to pursue its foreign policy goals. The two former bear the major emphasis in most cases unless there are issues in which China considers itself specifically involved, as with the Kampuchean problem. Where there is little the Chinese can actually do, media analysis receives the most emphasis. Concrete involvement with the Southeast Asian governments far outstrips substantive intergovernmental relations in other parts of the world, reflecting the typical Chinese pattern of paying most attention to areas geographically contiguous to it.

Conclusion

China's theories about the Third World have given China the *conceptual tools* with which to develop its policy toward various areas and issues of international politics. They also provide the *basis for rhetoric* when media coverage is required, or when attention in the media is the only course of action taken. With their component of antihegemony they have provided the rationale for Chinese criticism of superpower actions and policies, whether those of the United States or the Soviet Union. As one might expect, the Chinese use this overall conceptualization in different ways, depending on the situation. In general, the purpose of its position on the Third World in contemporary Chinese foreign affairs is to provide a vehicle for rivalry, which is of necessity often more rhetorical than practical. In addition, China uses its Third World policy to distance itself from U.S. policies that are repugnant to it or considered to be counterproductive.

To return to the two questions posed at the beginning of this chapter, it appears that China's current Third World policy is *consistent* with past practice, though *not identical* with it. The policy has evolved, as China itself has evolved. The concession that Third World nations do not lose their "credentials" by accepting aid from one or the other superpower is one of the most significant changes. In many ways, it brings Beijing's doctrine in line with its practice, since ideology has often been ignored in the past, as exemplified by the relationship with the Shah's regime in Iran or in the Chinese support of Pakistan when Bangladesh broke away. Beijing's current practices suggest that only in the most extreme situations, when China's national interest is directly involved, as in the case of Vietnam, will the Chinese leadership make an issue of an aid relationship with the Soviets. The ostensible Chinese tolerance of India's Soviet ties demonstrates how far Beijing can go to avoid making an issue of a situation it dislikes, in order to accomplish an important goal.

The Chinese policy emphasis in the 1980s is almost devoid of revolutionary ideology. This is demonstrated by the omission of references to China as a revolutionary model for development as well as by very low key support for revolution per se. This coincides with the across-the-board rejection of Marxist-Leninist ideology as a clear guide for practice and with movement toward a more pragmatic approach to both domestic and foreign policy issues.

China's Third World policy is far more than a side issue to Beijing's relationship to the two superpowers. It is in fact a set of concepts which define the parameters of those relationships. It is true that this policy does not hamper China in making decisions and adopting courses of action that are contrary to its conceptualization. But in general we can expect the Chinese to follow the line suggested by that conceptualization. The policy describes China's self-definition as antisuperpower, antihegemonist, a member of the Third World. Often this is no more than rhetoric. But it also indicates a genuine assumption that the Third World nations are important, that they can neither be ignored nor treated merely as pawns, that in some sense the future may indeed belong to them. Furthermore, it means that China's Third World policy is not totally an instrument relating to the superpowers. It is also designed to position China for a meaningful, dominant Third World role in the future, which the Chinese hope will be the means to a major world role. If we take this aspiration seriously, it may be possible to avoid misjudgments as to China's attitude or course of action on a number of issues. For U.S. analysts and policymakers in particular, to take it into account may produce a more realistic judgment as to how far the United States can depend on Chinese support for U.S. actions in relation to various Third World issues.

Endnotes

1. Mao Zedong, "China Is the Key," in Stuart R. Schram (editor), *The Political Thought of Mao Tse-tung* (New York: Praeger Publishers, 1969), p. 374.
2. Mao Zedong, "Stalin Is Our Commander!" in Schram, *Political Thought*, pp. 426–427; Mao, "On New Democracy," in *Selected Works of Mao Tse-tung* (Beijing: Foreign Languages Press, 1967), vol. II, pp. 343–347 and 364–365; and "On the People's Democratic Dictatorship," in *Selected Works* (Beijing: Foreign Languages Press, 1969), vol. IV, pp. 413–415.
3. Hua Guofeng, "Political Report to the 11th National Congress of the Communist Party of China" (August 12, 1977), in *Beijing Review*, no. 35, August 26, 1977, p 42.
4. *Chairman Mao's Theory of the Differentiation of the Three Worlds Is a Major Contribution to Marxism-Leninism* (Beijing: Foreign Languages Press, 1977).
5. Xinhua, September 7, 1982, in Foreign Broadcast Information Service, *Daily Report: China* (hereafter cited as FBIS/*China*), September 8, 1982, pp. K18–20.
6. Xinhua, December 5, 1982, in FBIS/*China*, December 7, 1982, p. K47.
7. Xinhua, May 31, 1984, in FBIS/*China*, June 1, 1983, pp. K14–18.
8. Beijing Zhongguo Xinwen She, January 13, 1985, in FBIS/*China*, January 15, 1985, pp. A2–3.
9. Beijing Domestic Service, January 30, 1983, in FBIS/*China*, January 31, 1983, pp. A1–7.
10. Beijing Zhongguo Xinwen She, January 1, 1984, in FBIS/*China*, January 3, 1984, p. A1.
11. Li Ning, "Intensified U.S.-Soviet Contention and International Tensions," *Guoji Wenti Yanjiu* (Beijing), January 13, 1984, pp. 1–6, in FBIS/*China*, March 2, 1984, pp. A2–11.
12. Shi Wuqing, "Superpowers Reach Military Balance," *Beijing Review*, no. 4, January 28, 1985, pp. 25–27.

13. Jia Yibing, "Always Stand with Third World," *Renmin Ribao*, September 18, 1984, p. 7, in FBIS/*China*, September 24, 1984, pp. A3–5.
14. Hong Kong AFP, March 28, 1985, in FBIS/*China*, March 9, 1985, p. D2.
15. Wang Naoqin et al., "Foreign Policy Trends of the New Reagan Administration," *Shiji Zhishi* (Beijing), no. 3, February 1, 1985, pp. 8–9, in FBIS/*China*, February 22, 1985, pp. B2–5.
16. Chen Feng, "Why 'Abstain'?" *Renmin Ribao*, August 2, 1985, p. 7, in FBIS/*China*, August 8, 1985, p. B2; Beijing Xinhua, August 7, 1985, *ibid.*, pp. I1–2; and Beijing Xinhua, August 3, 1985, FBIS/*China*, August 14, 1985, pp. B4–5.
17. "Inglorious," *Renmin Ribao*, September 9, 1984, p. 6, in FBIS/*China*, September 11, 1984, pp. B3–4 (quotes on p. B4). Also see Beijing Xinhua, October 17, 1984, in FBIS/*China*, October 18, 1984, pp. A4–5; and Beijing Domestic Service, March 28, 1985, in FBIS/*China*, April 3, 1985, pp. I1–2.
18. Yuan Shiyin interview with He Ying in *Shijie Zhishi* (Beijing), no. 9, May 1, 1984, pp. 6–7, in FBIS/*China*, June 29, 1984, pp. I1–4.
19. "Unjustifiable Provocations," *Renmin Ribao*, March 31, 1984, p. 7, in FBIS/*China*, April 2, 1984, p. B3; and "Veto," *Renmin Ribao*, April 15, 1984, p. 6, in FBIS/*China*, April 18, 1984, pp. B6–7.
20. Beijing Xinhua, September 18, 1984, in FBIS/*China*, September 19, 1984, pp. B2–3.
21. "Major Tension and Minor Relaxation in Central America," *Renmin Ribao*, December 19, 1984, p. 7, in FBIS/*China*, December 27, 1984, pp. J1–3.
22. Li He, "Evolution of the U.S. Policy Toward Latin America," *Shijie Zhishi* (Beijing), no. 15, August 1, 1984, pp. 5, 6, in FBIS/*China*, September 25, 1984, pp. B1–5.
23. See, for instance, "Roundup," *Renmin Ribao*, February 27, 1985, p. 7, in FBIS/*China*, February 27, 1985, pp. B1–2; and Beijing Xinhua Domestic Service, March 7, 1985, in FBIS/*China*, March 13, 1985, pp. B2–3.
24. Beijing Xinhua, March 21, 1985, in FBIS/*China*, March 21, 1985, pp. I1–2.
25. Wang Kun, "New Trends in Indian Diplomacy," *Renmin Ribao*, July 26, 1985, p. 6, in FBIS/*China*, August 5, 1985, pp. F1–2.

Chapter 5

INTERNATIONAL ORGANIZATIONS: CHINA'S THIRD WORLD POLICY IN PRACTICE

by Robert L. Worden

One manifestation of China's Third World policy is its behavior in international organizations. Championship of Third World causes in various international fora—the locus of power for Third World nations when working in concert—has been prevalent in the Deng Xiaoping era. Moral support to favored Third World initiatives and rejoinders to the developed world for its imperialist, colonialist, or protectionist attitudes toward the developing world are part of Beijing's international political behavior. More tangible demonstrations of substantive support to Third World causes are votes favoring key issues, various forms of aid, and leadership in the debate between the "North" (the industrialized states) and the "South" (the developing world). Indeed, a *common theme* found in every annual UN opening session address by Chinese representatives since 1971 has been the importance of Third World development and the effects of the First and the Second World's political, economic, and military policies on that development.

China's policies toward international organizations have evolved, as witnessed by the significant increase in memberships Beijing has gained internationally since achieving its seat in the

United Nations. Its view of the United Nations itself has changed from calls for revolutionizing the organization in the 1960s, to perennial calls for revision of the UN Charter in the 1970s, to the 1980s policy of consistently invoking the principles of the charter. All of these actions are done, however, with a clear view of Chinese *national self-interests*. A major incentive for joining more than three hundred nongovernmental organizations has been the *value* they can lend to China's economic modernization process. Third World solidarity notwithstanding, China is unlikely to compromise its own opportunities to gain the benefits available through international organizations, even at the expense of Third World causes. Thus, policy modification has been observed in areas such as raw materials cartels, in which China once saw great value, or support of the new international economic order, which has fluctuated in relationship to China's own participation in "old" international economic order institutions and conventions for its own sake without any appreciable benefits to the Third World.

The purpose of this chapter is to describe China's Third World policy in practice and evaluate how this policy has benefited the Third World in context with international organizations.

China's View of International Organizations

China's perspective on international organizations is part of its general foreign policy line. As it successfully established bilateral relations after 1949, the People's Republic embraced accepted practices of multilateral relations, which, in their modern, Westernized context, include a multiplicity of governmental and nongovernmental international organizations. China has eagerly joined international groups—with increasing frequency in the late-1970s and 1980s—usually in conjunction with declarations of equity for and solidarity with the Third World.

Its activities in international organizations have been conservative but optimistic. Seen as essential for the proper conduct of international relations, it is critical that all responsible nations belong to international organizations. Although China believes that international organizations could play a still more significant role in global and regional affairs, they *are* seen as providing a crucial forum for the expression of Third World viewpoints.

China's own approach to such organizations has ranged from antagonistic in the early days of the People's Republic when its memberships were limited to a few international Communist groups to an all-embracing stance in which Beijing's memberships in international organizations soared from just over 90 at the time of Mao Zedong's death in 1976 to nearly four times as many only five to six years later. Unlike the radical and disruptive situation that some felt would result from Beijing's presence in world affairs, China's representatives have been cautious and usually noncon-frontational but always, ostensibly, on the side of the Third World.

The adoption of this conservative modus operandi on the international scene has not meant that Beijing's representatives have been uncritical either of the organizations or certain member states. Traditionally, Beijing has declared that many of the major international organizations were controlled financially and through rules devised at their inception by the developed nations, particularly the Western industrialized countries led by the United States. The Soviet Union, too, has been seen as having interfered in international organizations but more often as a manipulator of those most closely associated with the Third World. Such selfish advantage of the superpowers and developed nations, in China's view, is to the detriment of the Third World nations seeking genuine national and economic independence.

View of Third World Organizations

Third World organizations per se are seen by Chinese policymakers as important in the ongoing struggle between the developed North and the developing South. In the Chinese perspective, exclusively Third World organizations are most effective when their members function with equanimity toward each other and in a coordinated fashion when dealing with the developed world. Like general membership organizations, it is believed that Third World groups are similarly disadvantaged by superpower interference, indirect control over funds in some cases, or general opposition to their goals. Interestingly, China's membership in exclusively Third World organizations is negligible.

As an integral part of its Third World policy, China has endeavored, since its seating in the United Nations in 1971, to use that organization and its specialized agencies as a major platform for the expression of views that it sees as supportive of the developing world. Beijing claims to have given a larger voice to Third World concerns from its vantage point in the United Nations, especially as a Permanent Member of the Security Council and as an important member of other UN bodies of key interest. Those of special interest to the Third World are the UN Conference on Trade and Development (UNCTAD), the UN Industrial Development Organization (UNIDO), and the UN Development Programme (UNDP).

Support of Third World Goals

Much of the rhetoric China uses in international fora is expressed in calls for the long-sought Third World goal of a new international economic order: a plan to achieve a stable and peaceful environment in which Third World states can develop their national economies by creating a more equal, interdependent relationship between North and South. China, while encouraging and participating in South-South cooperation, has tentatively presented itself as a bridge between the Third World and the industrialized nations with periodic calls for North-South dialogue. All such initiatives are designed to give the Third World a fair shake in their future development. Such initiatives, if brought to fruition, would be of immense benefit to China as well and help it achieve its strategic goals, as outlined by Robert Sutter in Chapter 2, without seriously hampering relationships with non–Third World nations.

If Third World goals are not realized, or only partially achieved, China still reaps the benefit of goodwill of Third World nations for having tried. As China modernizes and becomes increasingly integrated into the established international system—through broad-based international organizations—specifically Third World initiatives become less important to China. Even if the Third World becomes less important in its strategic plans, however, China's pro–Third World rhetoric is unlikely to change.

Many Third World leaders have expressed appreciation for China's support in international organizations, although a scepticism exists among some over China's motivations. Occasionally, some raise doubts, as noted in Chapter 1, about Beijing's Third World credentials, especially when they are viewed in juxtaposition with its motivations.

Joining International Organizations

By 1983, the People's Republic had joined some 340 international organizations, a sign of Beijing's commitment to the accepted international system and an indication of how domestic modernization needs have pushed the Chinese into joining a host of international professional, technical, and scholarly organizations. On the other hand, China has not joined such key Third World organizations as the Group of 77—the Third World coalition of some 120 countries in the United Nations; the formal Non-Aligned Movement; or the Organization of Petroleum Exporting Countries (OPEC). The fact that China's membership in exclusively Third World organizations is negligible, while membership in organizations open to all nations is on the rise, speaks loudly of China's pragmatic approach to global politics.

The factors mitigating against China's more active role in Third World groups—many of which Beijing voices approval—are much the same as those which keep China similarly distant from the United States and the Soviet Union. China's "independent foreign policy of peace" is applicable not only to balancing relations with the superpowers but in maintaining proper relations, in Beijing's perspective, with nations of the Second and Third Worlds as well. "Self-reliance" should not be read only in its anti-Soviet connotation but in the larger context of China's policy of not becoming attached to any nation or bloc of nations. Despite Marxist-Leninist modifications to the traditional Chinese world view, China continues to be wary of becoming too intimately involved or closely associated with any foreign nation, politically, economically, or militarily. This does not mean, however, that Beijing will not continue to give consistent and strong moral and financial support (when appropriate and within its means) to international organizations.

Pre-1971 International Participation

Since 1949 China has taken every opportunity to attend international conferences when it believed it could participate with equal status. China's inclusion in the Geneva Conferences of 1954 and 1962, the Bandung Conference of 1955, and the preparatory meeting for the Afro-Asian Conference in Cairo in 1957—all involving a variety of Third World issues—showed China's willingness to confer with other powers on international problems.[1] It was predictable, therefore, that Beijing, despite its bitterness over condemnation by the United Nations during the Korean War, would not behave differently from other members when, at last, it would be seated in the United Nations.

Rivalry with Moscow for influence among various Third World organizations was an important factor in China's international activities in the 1960s. Interparty polemics carried over into concerted Chinese efforts, throughout at least the early part of the decade, to offset Soviet advantages by promoting the differences between the developed world (including the Soviet Union) and the poor countries (including China). At meetings of such groups as the Afro-Asian People's Solidarity Organization, China's representatives sought to exclude the Soviets and to allow only "democratic organizations" from Asia, Africa, and Latin America. When resentment grew among Third World states not at odds with Moscow and it appeared China might not get its way, the Chinese threatened to withdraw. Events became particularly bitter when the First Conference of Solidarity of the People's of Asia, Africa, and Latin America (Tricontinental Conference) was held in pro-Moscow Havana in January 1966. The convocation of a similar conference in Beijing in 1967 was voted down by increasingly wary Third World bystanders in the Sino-Soviet dispute. The Beijing meeting site was transferred to Algiers but, mostly due to Chinese efforts to dissociate the Soviets from that meeting, the conference was never held. China became increasingly isolated from Third World groups.[2]

During this same period, China also expressed radical opinions about the United Nations. Indonesia's 1965 withdrawal from the United Nations was hailed by Zhou Enlai and was said to have "greatly advanced the struggle to reorganize the United Nations and terminate its manipulation by the United States and the other great powers." Chen Yi echoed these sentiments later in the year with his call for a "revolutionary United Nations." Indeed, one of China's goals for the abortive Afro-Asian Conference (to have been held in Algiers in 1965) was to seek an endorsement of its perception that the United States and other nations had manipulated the United Nations.

The fear of some nations, based on valid observations during the 1960s, that Beijing's radical and revolutionary impulses would obstruct the work of the UN Security Council (with its veto power) was not to be realized. Instead, China's new representatives after 1971, according to one observer, "quietly encouraged the use of a consensual approach whereby all discussion occurred informally before general agreement emerges through a draft resolution or a presidential statement, with or without a vote."[3]

International Organizations and the Open Door

Immediately following the establishment of the People's Republic in 1949, international organizations were put on notice by Beijing that it was the exclusive right of the Communist regime to be the sole representative of China. All memberships held by the former Republic of China were to be transferred to mainland representatives. Despite some minor successes, there was not to be any wholesale transfer for more than 20 years and only then with a fair degree of acrimony over Taiwan's firm insistence on its own exclusive representation.

The People's Republic, at the outset, was in contact at various levels with such major governmental organizations as the Universal Postal Union, the International Red Cross, and the International Geophysical Year. Even the United Nations maintained an information office in Shanghai until 1957, although its functions were obscure. China also was among the founding members of four international Communist groups: the Joint Nuclear Research Institute, the Fisheries Research Commission for the Western Pacific, the Organization for Collaboration of Railways, and the Organization for Cooperating in Telecommunications. During the 1950s, observers were sent to meetings of the Warsaw Treaty Organization and the Council for Mutual Economic Assistance, both under the heavy influence of the Soviet Union and thus, anathema to the Chinese after the 1950s.[4]

According to statistics kept by the Union of International Organizations in Brussels, in 1960, the beginning of a period of "self-reliance," Beijing could claim memberships in only 32 international organizations.[5] During this period China was crowded out of a host of groups which later become the "Communist front organizations," such as the Afro-Asian People's Solidarity Organization and the International Lawyers Association. Because of its increased ostracization from the international Communist community, Beijing was even more interested in joining international organizations as it competed for prestige with Moscow among newly independent nations and for allegiance of splintering Communist parties and leftist groups in the Third World.

By the eve of the Cultural Revolution and China's temporary retrenchment in international political participation, the People's Republic had increased its memberships to 59. The end of the radical stages of the Cultural Revolution, seating in the United Nations, and development of a moderate foreign policy, including that toward the Third World, brought still further changes.

At the beginning of the post-Mao era (1977 is chosen here for statistical purposes), 92 international organizations listed the People's Republic among their member states. With the acceleration of the economic modernization dictated by the new party line (starting in late 1978) and the formulation of an "independent foreign policy" (enunciated in 1982), a *quantum leap* in organizational affiliations was registered by 1983, with 338 international organizational memberships.

These memberships ranged from the United Nations and its numerous organs and specialized agencies to the Universal Esperanto Association. Representation can be found in such widely divergent organizations as the International Economic Association in Paris to the International Federation of Body Builders in Montreal; from the World Intellectual Property Organization to the International Brotherhood of Old Bastards in St. Louis, Missouri.

Data available through 1983 indicate the degree to which China has formally committed itself to international conventions. By that year, the Chinese had signed some 55 multilateral treaties and agreements. This is evidence of Beijing's commitment to the accepted international system and its willingness to adhere to international conventions in such areas as employment, remuneration, mariners' insurance, minimum age, forced labor, exchange of publications, drug abuse, and consular relations.

Participation in the United Nations. China's participation in the United Nations is pervasive. Within six months of seating in the UN General Assembly, the People's Republic had been recognized as the sole Chinese representative at all major UN organizations and specialized agencies. Yet, because of domestic political and foreign policy considerations, Beijing chose not to join all these organizations immediately, and some for not over ten years and then *only in line with its emerging economic modernization program*. Those Beijing did join in the early 1970s were UNCTAD, the Children's Emergency Fund, UNDP (membership in these three came automatically with General Assembly recognition), the Food and Agricultural Organization (FAO), the International Civil Aviation Organization, the UN Educational, Scientific and Cultural Organization (UNESCO), UNIDO, the World Health Organization, the Universal Postal Union, and the International Telecommunications Union. Involvement with the International Labor Organization, the International Atomic Energy Agency (IAEA), and the General Agreement on Tariffs and Trade (GATT) came much later.

Although not a member of the Group of 77, China's representatives, with increasing interest in the 1980s, participate in such Third World–dominated organizations as UNESCO and those of high Third World interest and activity as UNCTAD and UNDP. The Chinese also have participated in regional agencies of the United Nations, including the Western Pacific Regional Committee of the World Health Organization, the UN Economic and Social Commission for Asia and the Pacific (ESCAP, and its predecessor, the Economic Commission for Asia and the Far East), the ESCAP-sponsored Asia Reinsurance Corporation, and the FAO Conference for Asia and the Far East. Hosting of UN agency conferences in China became more frequent in the mid-1980s.

Organizations Joined Later. As part of their enhanced interest in obtaining foreign loans and investments, China's bankers were attracted to the Asian Development Bank as early as 1979 but did not express interest in membership until 1983. As with other international organizations, the issue of Taiwan's membership required resolution before Beijing would join. Despite support of China's membership by various Second and Third World members of the bank, the Taiwan issue remained an obstacle. The possibility of U.S. withdrawal should Taiwan be expelled and Taiwan's own donor status in the bank, coupled with the intransigence of both Beijing and Taipei, gave further life to the stalemate. While no longer insisting on Taiwan's expulsion, Beijing was willing to allow the model used for dual participation on the International Olympic Committee (IOC), which disallowed the use of the name Republic of China in favor of "Chinese-Taipei." The issue was eventually resolved by allowing Taiwan to be represented in the ADB under the name "Taipei, China."

General Agreement on Tariffs and Trade.   Because of its long-term policies on Third World development, Beijing was very slow to become involved with GATT. In 1983, however, while seeking protection for its own textile industry, China joined the GATT's 50-member Arrangement Regarding International Trade in Textiles (Multifibre Agreement) and its 1981 protocol of extension. In doing so, Beijing "reaffirmed [that its] participation in the arrangement [did] not prejudice its position regarding its legal status vis-à-vis the GATT." While implying GATT's continued unfairness toward Third World states, China said it wanted treatment equivalent to that accorded to other developing countries "with a similar level of economic development."[6] While becoming deeply involved in a dispute with the United States over textile restrictions—an issue of concern to other Third World textile exporters as well—China was able to have the GATT Textiles Surveillance Body examine the U.S. restrictions and request in late 1984 that they be lifted. The resolution of the case is an example of how China modified once principled stands in order to bring international pressure to bear on its behalf without any appreciable benefits for the Third World.

International Atomic Energy Agency.   In 1983 China joined the IAEA, in a sign of still further evolution of its nuclear policy and acceptance of international standards and obligations (such as voluntary inspections), an action sought by the Third World and nuclear powers alike. A move such as this not only manifested its own maturity in regard to the nuclear powers but was likely to allay Third World concerns, to some degree, over China's heretofore maverick status in the global nuclear affairs. It also eased the way for China's growing involvement in nuclear technology transfer both with developed countries such as the United States and Third World countries such as Pakistan and Brazil.

World Bank et al.   Similarly avoided in the first ten years of UN representation were the major financial institutions associated with the UN system. They are the International Monetary Fund (IMF) and the International Bank for Reconstruction (better known as the "World Bank"), with which is affiliated the International Development Association (IDA) and the International Finance Corporation. Together these organizations are considered in Third World circles as symbols of the "old international economic order." By the time of the Twelfth Congress of the Chinese Communist Party (September 1982), China had shed its reticence about participating in the programs of these agencies, in consonance with the new foreign policy line.

Nongovernmental Groups. China's participation in nongovernmental organizations, by far more numerous than governmental memberships (312 versus 26, respectively, by 1983), has been a *key part* of its economic modernization program. Critical to the program is the acquisition of foreign technology in virtually all fields of study and application. Domestic needs of the Four Modernizations (agriculture, industry, science and technology, and national defense) have *driven* the decisionmaking in joining a plethora of scholarly, technical, and professional associations. Generally they have been in the area of science and technology, mining and engineering, and trade.

Third World Groups. The impact of all this Chinese activity in Third World affairs has not been major. Among the current memberships with which China has some type of affiliations, only 30 have headquarters in Third World areas (including Hong Kong). Three others have headquarters in nonaligned Yugoslavia. Of the 30, very few, if any, can be considered exclusively Third World organizations. They comprise organizations whose headquarters happen to be Third World cities or are of a regional nature and deal exclusively with Asian problems or interests. One significant departure, beside China's interest in joining the Asian Development Bank, was its joining the Africa Development Bank Group in 1985. China's membership, as one of only 26 non-African members, was part of its intensified participation in international banking as well as an effort to accelerate economic relations with a major Third World area that harbors occasional suspicions about China's motives and methods. In the main, however, China's pro-Third World voice remains in the broad-based international organizations with headquarters predominantly in the Western countries (and Japan, Australia, and New Zealand).

Despite the high incidence of joining international organizations and its expanded activity in many sectors of international progress, China has much further to go. For a country of its size and complexity and desires of quadrupling the gross national product by the turn of the century, China does not yet rank among the major nations in terms of international participation. Developed countries such as France, West Germany, and even Belgium each have over two thousand international memberships. Very few

Third World countries are able to send delegations to more than a few hundred international organizations, although some of the more developed Third World countries, such as Brazil, Argentina, and India, have memberships in over one thousand international groups. As the 1980s progress, China will probably further expand the number of its memberships.

Even rival Taiwan, despite its many diplomatic setbacks since 1971, has actually increased its memberships, most notably in nongovernmental organizations. As of 1983, it held various levels of representation in nearly four hundred international organizations—more than Beijing's total.

The numbers game is not necessarily the most important contest in which China must compete but it is a further indication of its global participation and, thus, potential voice for, and competition with, the Third World.

Evolution of Attitudes Toward Third World Goals in the United Nations

The United Nations, the preeminent forum for Third World issues, is a favored vehicle for analysis of China's behavior in international organizations. Beijing's participation in the United Nations since 1971 is indicative of how Chinese policies on disarmament, decolonization, and development have been redefined and updated.

Disarmament

Despite earlier having excluded itself from negotiations on a world disarmament conference, in 1972 Beijing voted in favor of the Third World initiative to establish a 35-member Special Committee on the World Disarmament Conference. Additionally, China gave unequivocal support to Third World calls for nuclear-free zones around the world. In 1973, China signed Additional Protocol II of the Treaty for the Prohibition of Nuclear Weapons in Latin America—a substantial though guarded modification of its opposition to the Nuclear Non-Proliferation Treaty—and has sent observers to the periodic meetings of the Organization for the Prohibition of Nuclear Weapons in Latin America (OPANAL). By the late 1970s China had further adjusted its nuclear policy by issuing a call to the superpowers to significantly reduce their arsenals before the lesser nuclear states, like China, follow suit. These moves, and others such as joining the IAEA in 1983, were calculated, in part, to win favor in the Third World.

Law of the Sea

An apparent departure from its own territorial waters declaration was Beijing's avid support of a reform law of the sea, an initiative long sought by Latin American nations. China's support started with the UN Law of the Sea Conference in Caracas in 1974 and culminated with the signing of an international convention in Jamaica in 1982. Thus, through the vehicle of international organizations, China's posture toward a Third World area was "the most positive and fundamental note in the development of Chinese global policy."[7]

New International Economic Order

On development issues China adopted a rather "do as I say not as I do" position in international organizations. In earlier years, Beijing had emphasized its own success by means of self-reliance in developing its national economy. It held this means up, however, only as a "model proposition" for other developing countries. By the end of the 1970s, China's development model of self-reliance, once looked askance at by the world economic community, had come to be taken more seriously by those involved in development issues. Indeed, it was judged fortuitous that Beijing entered the United Nations prior to the inaugural process of establishing the new international economic order foundations, not only because of its huge population as a developing country but for the support, contributions, and elucidation it initially could give the process.

Beijing expressed wide support for the new international economic order in its own press and in statements before the United States, starting with Deng Xiaoping's watershed address before the Sixth Special Session of the UN General Assembly in 1974. China voted in favor of resolutions put forth by the developing nations for a redistribution of global economic resources; expressed support for the formation of regional economic raw materials organizations throughout the Third World; and sought the restriction or nationalization of multinational corporations, more equitable control over maritime and subsea resources, ways to stabilize the prices of

Third World products, and methods to renegotiate developing
countries' heavy debts.[8]

China's memberships in "old international economic order"
financial and monetary organizations and the extent of its involvement with trade and technological exchange with the developed
world were indicators of ambiguity in Chinese world economic and
development policies as the 1970s progressed. It also raised doubts
about Beijing's true feelings about the new international economic
order, which it had professed to support since the adoption of the
New International Economic Order Declarations, Programme of
Action, and Charter of Economic Rights and Duties of States by
the UN General Assembly in 1974. Some Chinese influence can be
found in these documents, but concepts in vogue in China in 1974,
such as resource sovereignty, antihegemony, and self-reliance,
were revised in the Deng period and Maoist enthusiasm for the
new international economic order became muted by the late
1970s. Self-reliance was replaced by concepts of global interdepen-
dence and division of labor and specialization, ideas once anathema
to Chinese ideologues. The sum of this evolutionary policy was, at
times, to put China at odds with the Third World community.[9]

Anti-Soviet Rhetoric

Overshadowing China's seemingly urgent pronouncements on numerous Third World issues was its increasingly heightened anti-
Soviet rhetoric as the 1970s progressed. This too caused concern
among Third World states observing China's use of the United
Nations as a stage on which to attack Moscow, particularly for its
alleged economic and military misdeeds in the Third World. Some
Third World nations, however, regarded China itself as acting like
a great power albeit one with limited resources to either establish a
genuine united front against the superpowers or aid other developing countries.

In the late 1970s, Beijing still argued diligently that the greatest
strategic threat to the Third World was the Soviet Union. During
the Eighth Special Session of the UN General Assembly in 1980,
China proposed that it was in the Third World's interest economically to stand up to the Soviets. Coming at a time when China
appeared to be moving closer to the United States and its traditional allies and muting its criticism of U.S. Third World policies,
as well as seeking concessionary interest rates and development

assistance from international organizations, Third World nations could not be blamed for looking askance at Chinese support of their causes.

Development Strategies

China's membership in the World Bank caused concern among Third World nations competing for the same kinds of consideration. There also was concern that unless low-cost IDA loans were granted on some basis *other* than a country's population, there was a strong possibility that China's share of IDA loans would come at the expense of other Third World members.

At one point in the new international economic order debates it was hoped by some that as China modernized it would make major input to world trade. As this hope faded, it became apparent in UN circles that China's support for the new international economic order and Third World development strategies was more rhetorical than anything else and did little to help its impoverished friends in Asia and Africa. Emerging with less radical policy in the late 1970s, China no longer sought radical solutions in world trade. Instead, despite its continued and detailed statements in international fora, China stood to gain little from the new international economic order. Indeed, with its centrally planned economy, China was seen as one of the emerging development poles, along with Eastern Europe and the Soviet Union, rather than with the traditional Third World states.[10] Third World interests appear to be sacrificed in favor of Beijing's anti-Soviet obsession, and by the end of the decade, China's credibility had been so affected that it was increasingly difficult for Beijing to rally Third World support to its causes.

Renewal of Third World Issues

In the early 1980s, Chinese support for the new international economic order and self-reliance were espoused anew. The revival came, however, in the form Samuel Kim calls a "dual track policy" of renewing development ties with the Third World through South-South cooperation while acquiring financial and technological assistance and investment from the advanced capitalist states.[11] China moved toward developing its "independent foreign policy" line of not being aligned or "attached" to any country or bloc of

countries. This line was given major articulation at the CCP
Twelfth National Congress in September 1982 and broached to the
world at the UN General Assembly Plenary Session the following
month.

The renewal of support for Third World issues at the United
Nations was accompanied by new levels and types of activities with
the Third World. These included increased numbers and quality of
bilateral exchanges, sponsored conferences in China on various
Third World issues, stronger support of the nonaligned movement,
increased diplomatic exchanges with Third World states, and
greater interest in reviewing foreign assistance programs.[12] After
the earlier failure of the October 1981 Cancun conference (a
summit in which China had placed high hopes), China joined other
Third World governments in fostering South-South cooperation.
This came in the form both of international conferences (China
hosted its own South-South conference in 1983) and the praising of
the merits of regional economic organizations. China began to see
South-South cooperation not as an alternative to the new international economic order, but as a way to that end through the means
of an exclusively but nonformal Third World vehicle. It was, for
China, a convenient means of expression of principles, an effective
mutual-help forum ("collective self-reliance") without the Third
World organizational structure that Beijing professes to support
but has not joined. Practically, the effect of all these moves was to
enhance Chinese credibility among Third World nations while
demonstrating to the industrialized nations that China could perform as a rational, reliable, and useful *link* between the developing
and developed worlds.

It was at this juncture that China embarked on a more vigorous
program of support of Third World issues in the United Nations
and its affiliated agencies. Beijing gave widespread support to the
new Law of Sea agreements, arranged to establish UN research
centers in China, and pledged increased funds in support of UN
projects, especially those facilitated by UNDP. As Kim has put it,
"By the end of 1983, China's differentiated opposition to both
superpowers had brought its global posture more or less in line
with that of the Third World." Its UN votes reflected China's
evolving independence from the two superpowers and its "symbolic rapprochement with the Third World."[13] Vigorous support of
Third World candidates for UN Secretary General and mediation
followed by staunch support of Argentina in the United Nations

during the Malvinas affair all helped China regain credibility among Third World nations.

Additionally, China showed increased interest in the basic economic principles espoused by the Group of 77. In 1983 China sent a nonvoting delegate for the first time to a Group of 77 ministerial conference held in Buenos Aires, and as the result of an invitation from the Chinese Ministry of Foreign Affairs, a Group of 77 delegation, led by its chairman, visited China in the same year.

The Central Role of the United Nations and Chinese Policy Projections

Chinese commentators see international politics as having undergone "tremendous and profound changes" since the establishment of the United Nations. They believe that an important indicator of such changes is that a large number of Third World countries have become a political force in the United Nations "not to be overlooked." Starting with few developing countries among UN members, Third World nations now comprise more than two-thirds of the membership. As Third World nations became more numerous and assertive in the United Nations, debates on various national liberation subjects were held and Third World nations were given a more equitable share of representation and decisionmaking in UN organs through a 1965 charter revision. Beijing sees the 1971 seating of the People's Republic of China as adding to the strength of the developing world in the United Nations. The 1981 election of Peruvian diplomat Javier Perez de Cuellar as UN Secretary General, a move strongly supported and abetted by Beijing after its first choice Third World candidate was successfully blocked by the industrialized countries, was seen as representing a major victory for the Third World in the United Nations.[14]

In this same Chinese analysis, the Third World began to overcome superpower influence in international organizations by "unit-[ing] to form a powerful force," and waging a "persistent and ceaseless struggle" in the United Nations against hegemony and power politics. Having won "one victory after another," the small, poor, and weak countries had forced the "veto lever of the superpowers" to have "gone out of order," allowing the Third World to raise its head full of confidence. In this contest, Beijing sees the nonaligned countries, the Group of 77, the Organization of African

Unity, the Arab League, ASEAN, and other regional organizations
playing an ever-prominent role in Third World affairs. Giving their
member countries of such organizations more confidence, their
representatives in the United Nations have acted in concert to
carry out measures such as blocking full status for South Africa,
condemning Israel and seeking its expulsion from the United
Nations, giving the Palestine Liberation Organization observer
status, and joining others in the UN General Assembly in demanding Vietnamese and Soviet withdrawals from Kampuchea and
Afghanistan, respectively. All this is said by Beijing's observers to
show that the United Nations of the 1980s has become "an important international forum for the Third World."

1971–1976

During the years since 1971, Chinese attitudes toward the United
Nations, in the context of Third World policy, can be seen in
statements made before that preeminent international organization. These attitudes show both what China sees as the proper
functions of the organization and what problems confront it. A
common theme found in all annual addresses made by Chinese
delegation heads to the opening of the General Assembly since
1971 is Third World development and effects of the developed
world's political, economic, and military policies on that development.

During the 1971–1976 period, when the People's Republic's
representatives were adjusting themselves to their new level of
international participation, China emphasized a number of areas
with concern to the Third World. With a new sense of equality in
global affairs afforded by UN membership, as well as a new sense of
power made available by permanent membership on the Security
Council, Beijing put considerable emphasis on pushing the Chinese model of self-reliance for dealing with thorny geo-political
and economic problems. It discussed the "significant role" of the
developing world in global affairs and the large number of Third
World issues—such as colonialism, economic disparity, maritime
rights, and using raw materials as a weapon—facing UN resolution.
The UN forum was used as another platform for opposing the
alleged enemies of the Third World: the United States and the
Soviet Union. China's spokesman during this period, Vice Minister
and later Minister of Foreign Affairs Qiao Guanhua, claimed that

there was increasing unity among Third World nations in the United Nations, a factor China approved of as they sought both multilateral aid through the United Nations and "auxiliary" bilateral foreign aid in the form of no- or low-interest loans, liberal or postponed repayment schedules, and no special privileges required of the recipient.[15]

In order to ameliorate what was seen as the domination of UN organs by the superpowers, a perennial call was made for the revision of the UN Charter. It was hoped that a revised charter would force the United Nations to "conform to the trend of the world" and help the organization to "regain its prestige and play its due role." The Soviets were specifically criticized in 1973 for proposing to UNIDO measures that would restrict sovereignty over natural resources to those nations capable of using those resources. In the area of disarmament, a favored Third World attention-getter, the Chinese criticized the United Nations for allowing speeches to multiply and resolutions to cloud the real issue—prevention of nuclear war. Although not willing itself to participate in a world disarmament conference (a position later changed) as proposed by other Third World countries, China did encourage the establishment of Third World area nuclear-weapon-free zones. Another issue, raised in virtually every annual address since 1971, was Beijing's ritual call for the dissolution of the UN Command in Korea, a Third World area containing a threat to China's national defense.

The most avid support for a Third World issue was China's declarations in favor of establishing a new international economic order, an issue previously discussed in detail.

1977–1982

Between 1977 and 1982, Beijing periodically invoked the Maoist Three Worlds Theory as a realistic analytical model. Third World development issues, however, were juxtaposed with heightened threats to Third World development by the Soviet Union. Linkages were noted between superpower contention in Europe and the world order needed for peaceful economic development. As the Soviet threat toward China itself increased—as perceived in indirect Soviet activities in Vietnam and Kampuchea and direct actions in Afghanistan—Beijing's representatives (Foreign Minister Huang Hua or, in 1981, Vice Foreign Minister Zhang Wenjin) called not for a revision of the UN Charter but its enforcement. Similarly, China invoked prior resolutions pertaining to Afghanistan and Kampuchea when criticizing Soviet transgressions. In a milieu of a steadily deteriorating international economic situation, China sought UN-sponsored conferences and offered support of Group of 77 and Non-Aligned Movement efforts toward the realization of the new international economic order.

Following the 1982 promulgation of the independent foreign policy line, Beijing noted the need for global negotiations and the creation of a more peaceful setting in which Third World states could develop their national economies. In his last UN appearance, Huang Hua announced China's expectation that the United Nations would "uphold justice and play a greater role in maintaining world peace and international security and in promoting the growth of the world economy." Despite China's own activism in UN groups and its apparent belief in the organization, Huang claimed that the UN system had failed because of the abuse of veto power, bypassing of the United Nations on important issues, and refusal to implement UN resolutions. China called again for all members to uphold, rather than revise, the charter.

Since 1983

The theme of upholding the charter, of making the UN system work, was continued in the subsequent period, starting in 1983 with the representation of the new Foreign Minister, Wu Xueqian. It was said that China, and by implication other developing countries which adhered to the Five Principles of Peaceful Coexistence, had always been in full accord with the UN Charter. When it was violated, the Third World suffered most. The failure to uphold the charter or implement resolutions had affected such Third World areas as Kampuchea, Afghanistan, Korea, the Middle East, southern Africa, Chad, Central America, and the Malvinas Islands.

Chinese support for the new international economic order was emphasized with the concept that Third World development was integrally linked to the world economy and international peace and security. If the Third World suffered economically, "the entire world economy [was] bound to suffer," said Wu in 1983. He criticized the developed nations for rejecting the Third World's "just positions" on development and specifically Third World proposals made at the Sixth UNCTAD. South-South cooperation, despite its limited progress, was raised as a temporary solution to the stalemated North-South dialogue in which China had put great hope earlier in the decade.

While expressing hope in the UN system, China continued to criticize it for becoming "rather flabby" in the settlement of important issues. Only by upholding the UN Charter could the ever-heavier responsibility for the maintenance of world peace and international security—needed for genuine global economic development—be realized.

Conclusion and Some Considerations for the 1980s

The main issue at stake in analyses of China's support of the Third World in international organizations is the degree of impact, of effectiveness, of benefit, to the Third World. How important is China's contribution? Is the moral support offered by China's representatives in international organizations always matched with concrete actions? Why has China abstained on occasion rather than vote in the United Nations for or against a controversial issue of importance to Third World colleagues? Are Chinese reductions in UN financial contributions likely to have a negative economic impact on the Third World and political repercussions for China? Are China's antisuperpower policies enunciated in UN councils incongruous with its pro–Third World policy and "independent foreign policy of peace"?

One veteran observer of China's behavior in the United Nations noted that, in its first decade of participation, Beijing's actions were "more symbolic than substantive, more political than functional."[16] The same observer labeled as "virtually negligible" Beijing's impact in the UN program area (but noted that China once voluntarily increased its assessments and was known for prompt and full payment, thus considerably strengthening the finances of the specialized agencies). Another observer concluded, however, after detailed analysis of UN voting records during the same period that China's positions were more favorable to the Third World than to Western nations.[17]

During its second decade of UN involvement, China's participation in that and other international organizations has evolved in accordance with its foreign policy line. While continuing to use international organizations as a Third World podium, a decade's experience has shown China how to avail itself of new development resources from the same organizations. In doing so, Beijing has become both champion and challenger to the Third World in direct proportion to its increased role in promoting Third World causes while seeking international development aid and protection of international conventions.

As a sign of less radical approaches to international politics in the United Nations itself, China replaced its perennial calls for charter revision with a moralistic defense of the charter itself. On the occasion of the 40th anniversary of the 1945 signing of the UN Charter, Chinese media and top leadership statements (including that made during a personal visit to the United Nations by Premier Zhao Ziyang) emphasized the importance, practicality, and vitality of the charter and, thus, of the United Nations itself. A United Nations Association of China was established, with the declaration that the United Nations was "an important front for the Third World to engage in diplomatic struggles as the organization has wide-ranging representatives, strong impact and a large-scale world forum."[18]

The 1980s present some apparent paradoxes in China's participation in international organizations. Rather than join the Group of 77, however, China has become a participant in such "old" international economic order establishments as the World Bank and the IMF. While once vocally promoting the causes and concerns of raw materials cartels, the Chinese have come to realize the diminishing effectiveness of the concept of raw materials as economic weapons against the industrialized world. Beijing, however, still encourages the work of international and regional groups such as the Andean Pact, the Arab League, OPEC, ASEAN, and others.

Since the late 1978 announcement that it would accept direct foreign loans and multilateral aid from various UN agencies, China began to receive UN technical and economic assistance from UNDP. China also revised its previously critical positions on the World Bank and the IMF as part of its strategy of seeking the cheapest possible loans and credit from foreign governments and international monetary and financial institutions as well as loans from foreign commercial banks. In assuming its seat at the World Bank and the IMF, China willingly submitted itself to stringent membership requirements once regarded as infringements on its sovereignty.[19] As China advances in this direction, has it left the

Third World behind or has it enhanced its own influence in ways that will provide long-term benefits to the Third World?

Other indicators of conflict in China's Third World policy include Beijing's failure to join the Group of 24, the Third World caucus in the World Bank. Its ability to reduce its own UN contributions while improving its eligibility for multilateral concessionary aid over the complaints of Third World nations is another problem area.

At a time of modest aid programs of its own while receiving close to $40 billion from UN, private, governmental, and intergovernmental sources, China must continue to reconcile its ideological support of Third World needs and demands. While cautiously guarding its own relationships with the World Bank and its affiliates, China has renewed its public support of Third World economic development and other causes in such international organizations as the World Bank, the IMF, the GATT, UNESCO, FAO, and the International Labor Organization (which Beijing finally joined in 1983 and, in doing so, assumed one of the ten seats reserved for "chief industrial states," something only Brazil and India of the Third World nations had ever done before[20]). Chinese reactions expressed in these fora, while giving a sense of Beijing's support for Third World causes and concern for the well-being of international organizations, indicate that China appears less aggrieved by strains between the industrialized nations and the Third World than has been the case in the past. A dichotomy between rhetoric and action in China's Third World policy continues unabated.

Endnotes

1. Ishwer C. Ohja, *Chinese Foreign Policy in an Age of Transition: The Diplomacy of Cultural Despair* (Boston: Beacon Press, 1969), pp. 71–72.
2. George Ginsberg, "The Soviet View of Chinese Influence in Africa and Latin America," in Alvin Z. Rubenstein (editor), *Soviet and Chinese Influence in the Third World* (New York: Praeger Publishers, 1976), pp. 206–207. Also see Carol R. Saivetz and Sylvia Woodby, *Soviet-Third World Relations* (Boulder and London: Westview Press, 1985), pp. 173–174.
3. Allen S. Whiting, "China and the World," in Allen S. Whiting and Robert Dernberger (editors), *China's Future: Foreign Policy and Economic Development in the Post-Mao Era* (New York: McGraw-Hill, 1977), p. 45.
4. Natalie G. Lichtenstein, "China's Participation in International Organizations," *The China Business Review* (Washington), vol. 6, no. 3, May–June

1979, pp. 28–29, provides the best background information on the subject for this period. The most rigorous analytical consideration of the subject is Samuel Kim's works as cited below.

5. *Yearbook of International Organizations, 1984/85* (Brussels: Union of International Organizations, 1984), table 3, p. 1432. There are divergent counts of China's memberships. One of Lichtenstein's sources, citing Beijing's own inventory, says that in 1957 Beijing was a participant in 64 international organizations. Even the UIO statistics cited in the 1984–85 edition are difficult to correlate with earlier editions, which may have included some confusion between mainland and Taiwan (Republic of China) memberships.

6. "China Admitted to GATT Group," *Beijing Review*, no. 1, January 2, 1984, p. 11.

7. Samuel S. Kim, *China, the United Nations, and World Order* (Princeton: Princeton University Press, 1979), pp. 169–171.

8. Harry Harding, "China and the Third World: From Revolution to Containment," in Richard Solomon (editor), *The China Factor: Sino-American Relations and the Global Scene* (Englewood Cliffs, N.J.: Prentice-Hall, 1981), p. 271. Harding's conclusions are based largely on Kim, *China, the United Nations, and World Order*.

9. Samuel S. Kim, "Chinese World Policy in Transition," *World Policy Journal* (New York), vol. 1, Spring 1984, p. 614.

10. Walter Goldstein, "Despair and the UN Development Decade," in Pradip K. Ghosh (editor), *New International Economic Order: A Third World Perspective* (Westport, Conn.: Greenwood Press, 1984), p. 338; and Samir Amin, "After the New International Economic Order: The Future of International Economic Relations," in Ghosh, *New International Economic Order*, p. 310.

11. Kim, "Chinese World Policy in Transition," p. 616.

12. John F. Copper, "China and the Third World," *Current History* (Philadelphia), vol. 82, no. 484, September 1983, p. 245.

13. Kim, "Chinese World Policy in Transition," pp. 610–611.

14. Chen Yichun, "The Third World Is Asserting Itself in the United Nations," *Renmin Ribao*, December 3, 1982, p. 6, in Foreign Broadcast Information Service, *Daily Report: China* (hereafter cited as FBIS/*China*), December 9, 1982, pp. A6–9.

15. The texts of UN General Assembly opening session speeches can be conveniently located in October or November issues of *Peking Review*, or *Beijing Review* since 1971.

16. Kim, *China, the United Nations, and World Order*, pp. 280, 329–330, 402. Also see Kim, "China and the Third World: In Search of a Neorealist World Policy," in Kim (editor), *China and the World: Chinese Foreign Policy in the Post-Mao Era* (Boulder and London: Westview Press, 1984). Pages 341–342 provide a bibliography of recent China–Third World analyses.

17. Trong R. Chai, "Chinese Policy Toward the Third World and the Superpowers in the UN General Assembly 1971–1977; A Voting Analysis," *International Organizations* (Cambridge, Mass.), vol. 33, no. 3, Summer 1979, p. 392.

18. Beijing Xinhua, July 17, 1985, in FBIS/*China*, July 18, 1985, p. A6. Also see Xinhua, September 26, 1985, in FBIS/*China*, September 27, 1985, pp. A1–2;

and Xinhua Domestic Service, September 27, 1985, in FBIS/*China*, September 30, 1985, pp. A1–2.

19. See good background information and projections through 1986 in Friedrich W. Wu, "External Borrowing and Foreign Aid in Post Mao China's International Economic Policy: Data and Observations," *The Columbia Journal of World Business* (New York), vol. XIX, no. 3, Fall 1984, pp. 54–60.

20. Kim, "China and the Third World," p. 181.

Chapter 6

EMERGING CHINA'S EFFECTS ON THIRD WORLD ECONOMIC CHOICE

by Bruce D. Larkin

China's vast, deliberate internal changes will, in all likelihood, lead to consequential change outside China. Given a China united, politically stable, at peace, committed to enter the modern world, and prepared to create the educational and economic preconditions to act extensively abroad, China will assume an increasingly salient global role. In global networks—networks of trade, communication, technology transfer, entrepreneurship, law, diplomacy, and policy—China increasingly speaks and deals. Beijing's premise is that the best guarantee of a role for China is perceptible common interest. Toward the external world, therefore, we may anticipate with some confidence a diverse, purposive, sustained, inventive, and cumulative quest by China for the terms and conditions that make joint interest more attainable. This will bring more Chinese into play abroad, commit more Chinese at home to production for external trade, and increase the *transactions* between Chinese and others. But even against the backdrop of more intense relations for all, China's engagement will grow in *relative* importance. A heightened stake in ongoing expectations will require political and legal defense. At every level, at the level of detailed commercial contracts and at the level of global rule-making, China will figure more prominently.

100

The principal external effects will be economic, and they will affect especially the Third World. Today China is still per capita resource-poor and a low-consumption society. There are real constraints on China's economic performance. Its population continues to grow, demanding food. Its trade as a portion of global trade is small. Its experience identifying, assessing, importing, and adapting new technology is recent. But the decisions which separate China today from the China of the 1960s have as their essence the quest for efficient production, trade, and profit, geared into the global economy. China injects itself into an already competitive world as a new actor.

The relevant question is not whether China's new role is for good or bad, but how Chinese participation will change the choices for others. The nonindustrial states of Asia, Africa, Oceania, and Latin America are more similar to China than are the Northern industrial states, are struggling themselves to achieve access to technology, and collectively export many of the same products on which Chinese sales will depend. For these reasons alone China's arrival matters to them.

We already see Chinese initiatives and their effects on the Third World. Three of the most important illustrate China's role as a country of low average income but economic ambitions:

1. China is selling widely and assertively to raise funds for the purchase of high technology from Japan and other industrial states. As a consequence, China is seeking market shares previously won by other Third World states.
2. China seeks a share of World Bank funding as a developing economy. Established World Bank borrowers must view China as a competitor, since the bank has not been able to obtain new funds proportional to the Chinese burden on the bank.
3. China is increasingly concerned with the institutions and regimes through which global access and economic exchanges are regulated.

The near-term consequences have been Chinese moral and political support for programs of institutional change, tending to support Third World hopes for a stronger voice.

In another sense, however, Beijing is the capital of a new industrial state. China's economy is dualistic: Its urban population of some 200 million supports a substantial industrial sector, and the rural 800 million remain an available Third World labor force. In the 1960s Dwight Perkins and Morton Halperin pointed out that in some respects the Chinese economy of 1965 was the equal of the German economy of 1935. China's aggregate capabilities, and capabilities in selected industrial fields, have grown since then.

Background to the 1980s

Since 1978 China's leadership has undertaken to remold the domestic economy, expand foreign trade, and secure membership for China in the world's major economic bodies. These steps serve domestic economic requirements and express a commitment to modernization.

China's population, projected to reach or exceed 1.2 billion by 2000, must be fed from a slender, intensively farmed arable base. Many material inputs are scarce, the infrastructure is burdened, and per capita industrial output is small. Recent harvest success does not contradict these facts.

As early as January 1975 Premier Zhou Enlai declared a new commitment to a policy of Four Modernizations, which was then taken up vigorously after the September 1976 death of Mao Zedong and arrest of the Gang of Four a month later. The uneasy coalition leadership of 1977–1978 committed itself, in a February 1978 speech by Premier Hua Guofeng, to a massive program of economic inputs and to ambitious 1985 farm and industrial targets. At year's end, however, Deng Xiaoping outmaneuvered Hua Guofeng and drew into the leadership core veteran economic specialist Chen Yun. Importation of whole plants and equipment undertaken in late 1978 was trimmed and stretched under Chen Yun's direction in successive retrenchments begun in 1979. This more disciplined use of imported technology coincided with moves to legitimize decentralized decisions in the domestic economy. Deng Xiaoping supervised a transition to new state and party leaderships headed by Premier Zhao Ziyang, who had experimented with incentive systems as a provincial party secretary, and CCP General Secretary Hu Yaobang, a long-time Deng protégé. Their mandate in turn is to guide a broad change in economic management, in part through markets and incentives. The focus of these policies in rural areas (locally in the late 1970s, broadly in

1983) was the "responsibility system" in agriculture, centered on household agriculture, and in urban areas (in 1984) in comprehensive management reforms.

In 1975 China practiced commune agriculture and directive industrial planning. Enemies of Zhou Enlai and Deng Xiaoping in the ministries concerned with foreign economic relations stressed the slogan "self-reliance" and criticized dealing abroad. Foreign debt was shunned. Foreign economic dealings with China were sharply constrained. China took part in only a few international economic bodies.

By 1985 much had changed. The responsibility system, more independent plant management and profit reinvestment, encouragement of exports, import of high technology, acceptance of some debt, experimentation with a variety of forms for foreign economic cooperation, and designating prosperity through work and entrepreneurship as a legitimate personal goal had transformed economic policy.

Declaratory Policy

China declares norms for economic relations with the Third World. A 1985 review by Zhang Weizhi, head of the Beijing Institute of International Studies, recalled Deng Xiaoping's remarks to the 1974 UN General Assembly Special Session on Raw Materials. These provide, in summary:[1]

- Adherence to antihegemony and the Five Principles of Peaceful Coexistence.
- National autonomy.
- Joint management of routine economic matters.
- Equality, mutual benefit, and exchange of needed goods.
- Support for raw materials exporters groups.
- Aid to respect sovereignty.
- Transference of effective, cheap, and convenient technology.

In China's schematic, normative design, what part is to be played by cooperation between China and Third World countries? The first point is that China has, since the early 1970s, defined itself as a Third World state.[2] Since China is a Third World state, China's relations are an instance of "South-South relations."

Cooperation with Third World Countries

In early 1984 China identified "some progress" in Third World
economies achieved "despite measures by the Western countries
to shift the economic crisis on to them." In October 1981 at
Cancun, the developing countries had taken a "cooperative attitude" on North-South economic relations and establishment of a
new international economic order but were rebuffed. There was,
according to the Chinese, "little possibility of reforming international economic relations through negotiations." Instead, Third
World states should strengthen collective self-reliance and develop
their national economies.[3] This formula preserved themes from the
1960s and 1970s.

China's sense of South-South relations is not confined to government ties or conventional trade. Large, widely trading corporations indigenous to developing countries are termed by one Chinese commentator "Third World transnationals." They are seen as
strengthening ties among Third World states and "promoting
South-South cooperation" but at the same time have some bad
effects on their domestic economies. For example, when they
invest abroad those funds are unavailable for investment at home.
Despite their drawbacks, he concluded, Third World transnationals "may eventually help bring about a change in the current
international economic order."[4]

In a major overview of Chinese foreign policy, the speech
delivered by Foreign Minister Wu Xueqian to the UN General
Assembly in 1984, China squarely followed the lead of the Group
of 77 in international economic policy. Wu cited "practical proposals" emanating from the group, confirmed commitment to the
1980 UN General Assembly International Development Strategy,
and supported—but only as a "long-term objective"—establishment of the new international economic order.[5]

Several months later Chen Zongjing, head of the Institute of
Modern International Relations, affirmed China's encouragement
of cooperation among Third World states. He noted obstacles,
including "shelving" of a proposal for a "South bank," and declared
that Third World states should "pay attention" to South-South
cooperation. He also cited the Lome Convention as an example of
a "wise measure" in North-South economic relations.[6]

In May 1985 a Chinese commentator forecast expanded South-
South cooperation, citing as reasons developing countries "becom-

ing more and more practical and skillful in carrying out South-South economic cooperation," expanding trade (especially in manufactures), and growth of joint ventures and financial cooperation between developing countries.[7]

Deng Xiaoping has told visitors that China will be a Third World country 50 years hence. More cooperation between Third World states will be seen in the future "although there is not much cooperation now."[8]

Trade: China as Competitor

China sells where it can to fund imports from the industrial states. The net effect is that buyers of Chinese goods in other Third World countries help to finance China's economic modernization. Table 6.1 gives export and import figures by region for 1982 to 1984.

We have a rough picture of China's trade if we imagine three major components: trade with industrial states (to buy their products), trade with the Third World (earning foreign exchange to buy industrial products elsewhere), and trade with Hong Kong. Sales to industrial economies yield about 46 percent of its 1982 export earnings. As to the triangular trade, only 18 percent of China's imports are bought from Third World countries (excluding Hong Kong), but they provide about 34 percent of export earnings (1982). Hong Kong appears as a major foreign exchange earner, and statistical series place Hong Kong among Third World entities as a major component of China's developing trade. But the Hong Kong trade includes flows of food at concessional prices and goods that are reexported in part to industrial states. In 1982 Hong Kong provided some 23 percent of Chinese exports but only 7 percent of imports.

There are credible economic reasons for the attractiveness of Chinese goods in Third World markets. They may meet consumer demands that would otherwise not be met or not met as cheaply. But because of Chinese policy—deliberate choices made by the leadership—Third World states are badly placed to sell to China. China allocates foreign exchange as a matter of policy, electing not to allocate foreign exchange for consumer goods analogous to its own export products in other countries. This does not mean that no foreign consumer goods enter the market, but that the leadership can still control the more important commitments of foreign

Table 6.1   Chinese Trade by Region, 1982–1984

	Million U.S. $		*Chinese Exports*		Percentage of all exports	
1982	*1983*	*Jan.–June 1984*		*1982*	*1983*	*Jan.–June 1984*
21864	22095	11857	World	100	100	100
10170	10297	5761	Industrial	46.5	46.6	48.6
799	975	524	to East	3.7	4.4	4.4
9370	9322	5237	to West	42.9	42.2	44.2
11688	11780	6088	Developing	53.5	53.3	51.4
998	848	403	Oil Export	4.6	3.8	3.4
10689	10932	5685	Non-Oil-Export	48.9	49.5	48.0
545	408	178	to Africa	2.5	1.9	1.5
629	526	272	to LA + Carib	2.9	2.4	2.3
7458	7880	4390	to Asia	34.1	35.7	37.0
5180	5796	3178	to Hong Kong	23.7	26.2	26.8

	Million U.S. $		*Chinese Imports*		Percentage of all imports	
1982	*1983*	*Jan.–June 1984*		*1982*	*1983*	*Jan.–June 1984*
18920	21312	11115	World	100.	100.	100.
14449	15837	8439	Industrial	76.4	74.3	75.9
1148	1332	720	from East	6.1	6.3	6.5
13301	14505	7718	from West	70.3	68.1	69.4
4362	5169	2501	Developing	23.1	24.2	22.5
359	318	178	Oil Export	1.9	1.5	1.6
4004	4851	2323	Non-Oil-Export	21.2	22.8	20.9
253	302	144	from Africa	1.3	1.5	1.3
865	1486	468	from LA + Carib	4.6	7.0	4.2
2693	2814	1605	from Asia	14.2	13.2	14.4
1314	1709	1130	from Hong Kong	6.9	8.0	10.2

SOURCES: IMF, *Direction of Trade*, December 1983, July 1984, and November 1984.

exchange. How to manage foreign exchange is an issue analogous to those of factory management and domestic input allocation. In any case, despite restrictions, China is something of a market, and a growing market, for imports from other Third World states.

Third World states are attentive to trade imbalances, and there is ample evidence of pleas to China from Third World states to "balance" trade. A trade deficit is more tolerable, of course, when it is small as a proportion of all exports, as is the case for many of

Table 6.2 Chinese Trade, 1977–1984

	Chinese Exports (fob) and Imports (cif) U.S. $ billions							
Year	1977	1978	1979	1980	1981	1982	1983	1984
Exports	6.8	9.7	13.7	18.1	21.5	21.9	22.1	24.4
Imports	6.3	10.9	15.7	19.5	21.6	18.9	21.3	25.5
	Chinese Exports and Imports as Percentages of World Exports and Imports							
Year	1977	1978	1979	1980	1981	1982	1983	1984
Exports	.7	.9	.9	1.0	1.2	1.3	1.4	1.4
Imports	.6	.8	.9	1.0	1.0	1.0	1.1	1.3

SOURCE: *Far Eastern Economic Review*, 28 February 1985, p. 99, citing IMF, *Direction of Trade Statistics Yearbook*, 1984.

China's trading partners in the Third World. This is not to argue that trade deficits do not matter, but that if China's trade becomes a greater proportion of world trade, as trends moving from the very low levels of the early 1970s suggest, proportional imbalances will be less tolerable to Third World trading partners. The trend in Chinese trade as a proportion of world trade is shown in Table 6.2.

Accounts of the 1980s report growing concern among Third World exporters that Chinese exports will come to compete with their products in their traditional markets. For example, dispatches published in February 1985 by *Far Eastern Economic Review* correspondents reported:

> *Senior [Malaysian] policymakers realize that [Beijing's] export drive gives China an entirely new external dimension for Malaysia. While in security terms they continue to describe China as "the long-term threat to Southeast Asia," the prospect of China as a powerful, free-trading economic adversary is possibly even more alarming. They foresee a danger of a drive by China into markets where Malaysia is also selling, and of their own strong export performers—electronics, textiles and clothing products—taking a drubbing from Chinese competition later in the decade. . . .[9]*

They say that a significant part of the Thai maize trade has been lost to China, quoting an unnamed senior executive of the Thai Board of Trade that "it looks like Thailand's traditional markets in Southeast Asia may soon be [completely] taken over by China."[10] Of India, the *Far Eastern Economic Review* asserted:

China has successfully blunted India's export thrust in a number of third-country markets, in a range of products. A study by the Indian Council for Research in International Economic Relations noted that China has been elbowing India out in Western markets for cotton fabrics, yarn and light-engineering goods. Chinese exports of cotton fabrics to the major markets of the West virtually doubled during the period 1978–82, while imports from India fell. China's share of the industrial-fastener market quadrupled during 1978–82, while India's share fell to just 35 percent of pre-survey levels. Price cutting by China was seen as the most important factor.[11]

But this competition did not impede the August 1984 signing of a trade agreement in which China and India accorded each other most-favored-nation status.[12] Finally, the *Review* cited an academic study, which concludes as follows:

Chinese exports of textiles, floor coverings, clothing and footwear would have a substantial effect on world markets by the end of the decade, crowding out competitors and creating protectionist demands. If China attained its production-growth target of 7 percent a year, shares of world markets could range from 6 percent for footwear to 28 percent for textiles.[13]

One can imagine, however, that the authors realize that sustained straight-line production growth will almost surely be defeated by its own consequences, as it provokes importers and competitors to the full range of remedies on which they can call.

Hong Kong: A Special Case

The Hong Kong trade poses a special problem for the analyst, since Chinese exports to Hong Kong are such a large proportion of Chinese exports yet are linked to the special position of Hong Kong. The December 1984 signing of an agreement between China and the United Kingdom governing Chinese resumption of authority in 1997 suggests the need also to consider China's trade with Hong Kong as internal trade. The principal characteristics of the Hong Kong trade are these:

- Much of the trade is food to feed the people of Hong Kong. This is best understood as internal trade, although it now earns foreign exchange.
- Some of the trade is for reexport. To the extent that it goes to

Third World countries, it is not distinguishable from products shipped directly. Reexport trade includes, according to many reports, a quasi-surreptitious Chinese trade with South Korea, and some traffic with Taiwan.

- After 1997 it will be necessary to make judgments on how Hong Kong exports to other states are to be regarded. For example, one might consider China's ability to compete in consumer electronic goods to be suddenly enhanced by the manufacturing capabilities of Hong Kong.
- The principal change will be to connect China's productive capability more intensely with the world of transactions. China's capacity to compete with other suppliers in Third World markets will become even greater as Hong Kong middlemen develop their special relationships with Chinese sources.

Foreign Exchange Reserves

During the early 1980s China has been building its foreign exchange reserves. Reported reserves are shown in Table 6.3. In 1984 a Japanese analyst termed China—with foreign debt at the time of about $3 billion and reserves exceeding $14 billion—a "most creditworthy nation." Only West Germany, Saudi Arabia, Japan, Italy, and France held more foreign currency. It was probably in 1982 that China became a net lender. However, concerned that its reserves might jeopardize access to long-term low-interest funds from international lenders, China has taken pains to describe the reserve surplus as only temporary.[14] Beijing's caution may be justified and its description correct. In the latter

Table 6.3   Foreign Exchange Reserves, 1981–1985

		Year-End			
	1981	1982	1983	1984	May 1985
U.S. $ million	4,700	11,100	14,300	—	19,000

Source: 1981–1983: *Beijing Review*, no. 19, May 7, 1984, p. 12. May 1985: *Far Eastern Economic Review*, May 23, 1985, p. 70. China has said that it then experienced a sharp drop in its reserves in 1985.

part of 1985 China's reserves declined by several billion dollars. The wish to import has been stemmed not by market forces but by official limits, forced by the inability of the domestic economy to absorb greater investment without politically unacceptable dislocation or provide the infrastructure required by large-scale technology imports. As those requirements are set in place, and as the habit of decentralized decisionmaking takes firmer hold, however, the pressure to import will mount again. There seem to be cyclic processes at work. Nonetheless, China's position is very different from that of Third World states that have committed substantial fractions of foreign exchange earning to debt service.

New Ventures: Antarctica and Maritime Zones

As China enters global competition, the world's sovereignties are jockeying for access to the only remaining economic resources not yet under exclusive sovereignty: the seas, Antarctica, and space. Steps already taken by Beijing declare that China intends to have a share. As in other matters, China in part makes common cause with other less-industrialized states, and in part will be sharing only at their expense.

China encouraged Third World initiatives in the UN Law of the Sea Conference. One major consequence of that conference was to confirm the legitimacy of vast coastal economic zones, and a second—disputed by the United States—to bring forth an international mechanism to regulate and undertake seabed mining beyond the limits of national jurisdiction. China has stressed peaceful settlement of conflicting ocean claims, but in reality is postponing steps to settlement because the conflicts it would face would engage Vietnam and South Korea, not to mention Taiwan.

In 1984 China undertook its first independent Antarctic expedition. Deng Xiaoping sent it off with a plaque inscribed "Towards peaceful utilization of Antarctica by humanity," and in early 1985 two members of the expedition planted the Chinese flag at the South Pole. One Chinese commentator noted that "Third World countries are . . . concerned about the exploitation of resources there." Although China acceded to the Antarctic treaty in May 1983, the commentator noted that the treaty imposes "undue limitations on . . . developing countries."[15]

Major Commodities

China exports four bulk commodities with implications for other Third World countries: oil, tea, tin, and tungsten (wolfram). Oil and tin are the subject of price-maintenance agreements among suppliers. Beijing has attended discussions with other tea exporters, and in 1984 an exporters' group was said to be "likely" to be formed by India, China, and Sri Lanka.[16] China is also a buyer of copper and therefore follows with interest copper exporters' activities. The bulk commodities are distinguished from clothing and textiles by their relatively simple character and limited sources: Although clothing and textiles are a major Chinese export, relative ease of production and low entry cost pit low-wage states against each other, and place industrial-state buyers in a commanding position from which they grant quotas for stipulated fractions of the market. The opportunity for producer regulation of the market is small.

Oil remains the prime example of producer price management. In the early 1970s OPEC demonstrated that oil suppliers could achieve significant earnings increases by selling at agreed prices. This capacity depended upon OPEC members having a large market share and users having no adequate counterstrategy. China benefited from OPEC's creation by selling rather small quantities of crude oil (typically less than 10 million metric tons), largely to Japan, at prices at or near OPEC prices.

Although at one time there were speculations that China would become a major oil seller, falling supply from established fields, delays in bringing new fields to production, and internal Chinese demand have combined to limit Chinese exports to a fraction of the speculated amounts. On the other hand, China has been careful to rely on its abundant coal deposits and avoid import dependence on oil. As a result China has remained largely insulated from the world oil market. China has had negligible effect on OPEC's ability to maintain, or inability wholly to maintain, agreed prices.

Chinese commentary on OPEC credits OPEC with "stabilizing" the international oil market. Beijing observes that self-serving policies opened the way for "Western oil companies" to hoard and then sell reserves and that OPEC rose to the occasion, working out production quotas and stabilizing price.[17] China fails to provide a convincing explanation of OPEC's actual encounter with glut.

Nonetheless, cyclic resurgence of global oil supply, forcing the price down, works against Chinese export earning.

Beijing's position in tin and tungsten, however, is more significant. In the 1970s China reportedly agreed to withhold some tin shipments from the market at a time when other exporters were hurting. China remains attentive to the Malaysian market and aware that its commercial practices can affect price. The record in the early 1980s, however, is that the International Tin Council's buffer-stock operations have suffered heavy losses, not encouraging for price-maintenance strategies. Any Chinese sales abroad help depress price and therefore the profit of other tin exporters. China's production is about 7 percent of world production.

In tungsten China's role is still more important. A very large fraction of tungsten production—in 1983, 26 percent—is of Chinese origin. The Soviet Union produces about 19 percent; of Third World states, only Bolivia, with about 6 percent, and South Korea, with about 5 percent, are significant producers. Chinese market operations will continue as a major influence on price.[18]

China has not abandoned at least the appearance of interest in commodity producers' organizations, but there is no echo of the rather aggressive language of the early 1970s or a sense that China expects the OPEC model to be extended (as some producer states once hoped it would be) to a panel of 18 major commodities.

Labor Export

In the latter 1970s China undertook to emulate those countries, especially South Korea and the Philippines, that had earned foreign exchange by dispatching workers abroad. In October 1983 China reported that 42 Chinese companies were undertaking projects abroad and that 30,000 Chinese workers had been sent abroad to perform the contracts.[19]

Aid

In the first six months of 1983 China signed 18 foreign aid agreements, bringing the total entered into with the Third World since 1980 to 402. Sixty-four countries had been receiving Chinese aid; the new agreements brought the number to 77. But the scale of projects was reduced. In effect, China appeared to be striving for symbolic projects widely distributed.[20]

In 29 countries in early 1984, "more than" 800 Chinese agro-technicians conducted aid activities. Their work ran from Chinese strengths: grain, sugarcane, vegetables, and fish raising.[21] The small total of personnel and the large number of countries among which they are scattered suggest that many of these projects are minimal symbolic gestures. Nonetheless, they appear to have made a generally favorable impression and encouraged the understanding that China, despite her own limits, identifies with the needs of Third World states.

The World Bank and the International Monetary Fund

The World Bank, the IMF, and the International Fund for Agricultural Development supplied China with significant funds in the 1979–1984 period. They were among the sources of more than $10 billion borrowed from abroad during that period; China also repaid some $6 billion.

Another prospective source of foreign exchange is the Asian Development Bank (ADB). Whether Beijing would become a participant in the ADB was not resolved at the eighteenth meeting of its governors (29 April to 2 May 1985); Beijing's application foundered on disputes about the conditions under which Taiwan might continue to function within the ADB. China complained of the "uncooperative attitude from certain parties over the question of China's membership."[22]

Beijing took its seats in the World Bank and the IMF in 1980. It was soon the beneficiary of monies raised by the IMF through the sale of gold (undertaken from 1976 to 1980): Of $3 billion to be shared among developing countries, China received low-interest loans of $309 million in the first round of distributions.[23] A second allocation was authorized in 1985.

China's borrowing from the World Bank had, by 1985, reached nearly $1 billion in a year. The International Finance Corporation, a World Bank affiliate, was venturing into a Chinese project in 1984, and China was an evident candidate to borrow from the bank's second affiliate, the International Development Association (IDA). World Bank President A. W. Clausen stated in April 1984:

We are encouraging China to borrow more, from both the World Bank and commercial banks. But the Chinese are rightly reluctant to accumulate debt too rapidly, especially in view of the volatile debt situation of so many other countries. The advanced industrial countries have strong reasons—commercial, political, and humanitarian reasons—to assist China in reaching its development goals. But our continued inability to provide much IDA assistance is, unfortunately, likely to limit the potential role of The World Bank in China.[24]

At stake here was the danger that Chinese claims would take funds away from traditional IDA clients. An alternative to cutting smaller slices was to enlarge the pie. To that end the bank sought $16 billion in contributions to IDA-7, the seventh IDA replenishment. The United States, however, confined its contribution to $750 million per year, a total of $2.25 billion over three years, which by formula fixed the total figure to be provided by all donors at $9 billion. Indications in September 1984 were that approximately $1.8 billion would be divided between China and India over the three-year term, or perhaps less.[25] China's prospects for support from IDA are therefore substantially below expectations, and China will compete with traditional borrowers. This does not seem likely to change: In his 1985 budget message U.S. President Ronald Reagan said the United States was "not budgeting at this time" for any future replenishment after its commitments to IDA-7 were exhausted.[26]

Beijing's quest for advantage did not lead it to silence with respect to practices that other interests required it to criticize. Of IMF-sought debtor state austerity programs, a mid-1984 Chinese commentary said that they "have actually forced the debtor countries to tighten their belts to meet payments and pushed them further into debt crisis from which they no longer recover."[27]

In December 1983 China joined the GATT Multifibre Agreement, underscoring that it would continue to compete for access to textile markets in importing states. To the extent that advantages are accorded within the framework of the Agreement by level of economic development, China expected treatment "equivalent" to that of states of similar level.[28]

What Has Become of the Chinese Model?

How does China view the economic situation in the Third World? A review of African economies by two researchers at the Beijing

Institute of International Studies asserted that since 1980, Western countries have shifted their "economic crisis" onto African states, with four results: slowed economic growth, worsened exports, more acute agricultural problems, and a heavier debt burden. In response, the Chinese researchers wrote, African states have adopted measures which are stated to appear strikingly like those China has adopted: reducing the scale of capital construction, giving importance to agriculture, "reorganizing state enterprises and improving their management," enlarging the role of private business, and slowing nationalization.[29]

When in the early 1960s the Chinese Communist Party strove to find and applaud examples of revolutionary struggle, Algeria was repeatedly cited as a progressive example. Twenty years later, Chinese objectives having changed, Beijing identifies as keys to Algerian economic success policies mirroring Chinese internal economic guidelines: cancellation of nonpriority and unprofitable investment projects, decentralization of state-run enterprises, and the private sector operating in tandem with the state-run economy.[30] Algeria is not the only country cited in this vein, but the irony is stronger.

Conclusion

The Third World has become, in its various aspects, a market, a competitor, and a qualified and sometime partner for China. China cannot escape the ambiguity of purpose inherent in complex relations: Beijing continues to champion joint Third World interests against the industrial states but at the same time is a partner of Japan, Western Europe, and the United States in essential trade and in a shared commitment to stable global conditions.

Nor is China alone in changing. Other Third World states are moving to become more deeply engaged participants in global trade, communication, and decisionmaking. China appears to be approaching a fork in the road, becoming more like those Third World states that are large in themselves, industrial, and regional powers, and less like the states trapped in poverty and dependence. This will certainly *intensify* China's relations with the Third World states of Asia, large and small, and will create the *possibility* of common cause with other states—Brazil, Mexico—that are in some sense similarly placed.

Over the longer term, if present trends continue, the following impacts will result:

- China's importance will increase as a supplier to Third World states, in an array of products including those embodying intermediate technologies.
- In turn, increasing choice for Third World buyers will result.
- Chinese competition with Third World states as suppliers to third parties will increase.
- Chinese competition will increase in services, including ocean shipping and, gradually with time, more esoteric facets of international trade and finance.
- Pressure will sharpen on international granting and concessionary lending institutions, and on the services of other international organizations.
- Political pressure by Third World states will be felt for Chinese purchases more nearly equaling Chinese sales in their countries.
- In Southeast Asia concern will grow about economic dependence on China and the role overseas Chinese may come to play in enhanced economic relations.

There are several more problematic but intriguing possibilities: China may dedicate research and engineering directly to make "intermediate" products effectively meeting Third World requirements; China's expanding role may induce other Third World states to cooperation so that they can, with combined resources, create Third World alternatives to China in the quality and array of products; and China may prove more successful than others in birth limitation, inviting imitation. In fact, how China comes to be assessed in the Third World may depend more on Beijing's success or failure in population policy than on any other factor. Failure to restrain population growth will depress the per capita level of living and place an even heavier burden on China's slender arable land; China's ambitions will be constrained. On the other hand, if others cannot control their populations and China can, the Chinese model will be more salient in the Third World. The final irony then would be that China could achieve through practical policy acknowledgment that it offered an apt example, an acknowledgment it could not win by ideology in the 1950s and 1960s. Too many uncertainties lie ahead to predict how others might judge a "Chinese model," but there is little question that China's ongoing experience will be observed, assessed, and—where successful—drawn upon.

Endnotes

1. Zhang Weizhi, "Independence Is the Basic Canon: An Analysis of the Principles of China's Foreign Policy," *Beijing Review*, no. 1, January 7, 1985, p. 19. The Five Principles were reaffirmed by Zhao Ziyang at a Beijing forum on July 8, 1984, and in an article by Han Nianlong, adviser to the Ministry of Foreign Affairs, "Five Principles Guide China's Diplomacy," *Beijing Review*, no. 31, July 30, 1984, pp. 17–20. Han also recalled the four principles Zhao enunciated during his 1982–1983 African tour: "equality and mutual benefit, stress on practical results, diversity of forms, and common progress."

2. Zhang, "Independence Is the Basic Canon," states: "Socialist China belongs to the Third World. China believes that safeguarding Third World interests is its international obligation at all times. It firmly supports their struggle for independence and economic development, and is always improving the cooperation with them and encouraging unity."

3. Tan Feng, "Overcoming Economic Difficulties," *Beijing Review*, no. 7, February 13, 1984, pp. 14–16. China continues to give at least declaratory approval of the new international economic order. Also see Ti Fu, "North-South: Problems of Economics and Politics," *Beijing Review*, no. 26, June 25, 1984, p. 14, which terms reforming North-South relations and "reforming the old international economic system" to be "top priority."

4. Zhang Zuqian, "Third World Transnationals on the Rise," *Beijing Review*, no. 11, March 18, 1985, pp. 16–19.

5. Text of Wu's speech, "China's Stand on World Development," in *Beijing Review*, no. 41, October 8, 1984, pp. 16–18, 23–25. Wu declared China's readiness to "join the other developing countries" in unremitting efforts to achieve a new international economic order and also applauded South-South cooperation.

6. Chen Zongjing, "South-South Ties Grow Stronger," *Beijing Review*, no. 2, January 14, 1985, p. 18.

7. Wang Hexing, "Developing Countries Step Up Co-operation," *Beijing Review*, no. 19, May 13, 1985, pp. 18–19.

8. From Deng Xiaoping's talk with Ecuadorean President Osvaldo Hurtado, May 17, 1984, in "China Always Belongs to Third World," *Beijing Review*, no. 22, May 28, 1984, p. 9. The basic Chinese formula, stated succinctly in this talk, is that "two basic questions" faced the world: "opposition to hegemony and defending world peace" and the North-South question.

9. "Threat or Challenge: Asian Countries' Response to Peking's Trade Push," *Far Eastern Economic Review* (Hong Kong), February 28, 1985, p. 98.

10. *Ibid.*, p. 100.

11. *Ibid.*

12. "The Week: China," *Far Eastern Economic Review*, August 30, 1984, p. 7.

13. Untitled paper by Chris Findlay with Prue Phillips and Rodney Tyers, cited

in Hamish McDonald, "Ahead of the Crowd," *Far Eastern Economic Review*, February 28, 1985, pp. 99.

14. Imai Satoshi, Director, China Section, Japan External Trade Organization, in *JETRO Newsletter* (Tokyo), no. 49, 1984, pp. 5–8.

15. Mu Youlin, "China Sends Expedition to the Antarctic," *Beijing Review*, no. 50, December 10, 1984, pp. 4–5.

16. Mohan Ram, "Tea-Exporting Nations Plan to Get Together," *Far Eastern Economic Review*, September 27, 1984, p. 10. In 1982 China exported 13 percent of world tea exports, and India and Sri Lanka together, 45 percent. See *1984 Commodity Year Book* (Jersey City, N.J.: Commodity Research Bureau, 1984), p. 343.

17. Jiang Hong, "Cooperation Stabilizes Oil Market," *Beijing Review*, no. 14, April 2, 1984, pp. 15–16. Also see Zhang Zhenya, "OPEC: Producers Battle Oil Price Cuts," *Beijing Review*, no. 46, November 12, 1984, p. 13.

18. *1984 Commodity Year Book*, p. 356.

19. Xinhua, October 8, 1983 as cited in *China Aktuell* (Hamburg), October 1983, p. 642/12. Note that the 30,000 workers were probably not abroad simultaneously.

20. *Ibid*. A good summary of current Chinese aid policy can be drawn from the agreements signed by Vice Premier Tian Jiyun during visits to Sierra Leone, Benin, and Liberia. China was to provide "interest-free loans to be used mainly for projects already under construction, to consolidate projects now in operation, and to build some small and medium agricultural, industrial, cultural, and health projects." See "Economic Ties with Africa Grow," *Beijing Review*, no. 52, December 24, 1984, p. 10. Tian also visited Nigeria, Togo, and Mali. Examples of some projects follow.

    Guyana: a joint China-Guyana undertaking in fisheries, for which China will provide the trawlers and some other requirements in return for a 49 percent share, reached at least the letter-of-intent stage. Note that this offers the prospect of commercial return and is an Atlantic venture. Xinhua, May 15, 1984, in *China Aktuell*, May 1984, p. 275/3.

    Sudan: On December 15, 1984 China signed a loan agreement with President Nimeri of the economically embattled Sudan. See "Sudan President Holds China Talks," *Beijing Review*, no. 52, December 24, 1984, pp. 9–10.

    Tanzania: The much troubled TanZam Railway reportedly made a $6 million profit in fiscal year 1983 according to Xinhua, September 14, 1984, in *China Aktuell*, September 1984, p. 544/2. A compact but informative summary of this most ambitious Chinese aid project is in *China Aktuell*, November 1983, pp. 708/8–9. During a visit to China by Tanzania's Prime Minister Salim A. Salim, China extended a commodities loan. See "Relations Satisfy Tanzania Leader," *Beijing Review*, no. 40, October 1, 1984, p. 7.

21. Lu Yun, "China's Agro-Technology Aid Abroad," *Beijing Review*, no. 9, February 27, 1984, pp. 26–27.

22. "A Tale of Three China's," *Far Eastern Economic Review*, May 16, 1985, pp. 63–65.

23. Clyde H. Farnsworth, "I.M.F. Plans to Recycle Aid for Poorest Nations," *New York Times*, May 29, 1985, p. D9.

24. A. W. Clausen, speech to the Los Angeles World Affairs Council, April 25, 1984, World Bank, Washington, D.C.
25. See an excellent discussion in Robert Manning, "Soft Loans: IDA–7 Makes Do," *Far Eastern Economic Review*, September 27, 1984, pp. 82ff., and a detailed report on China's relations with the World Bank in *ibid.*, pp. 97ff.
26. "Reagan Warns of End to IDA Contributions," *Far Eastern Economic Review*, February 14, 1985, p. 8.
27. Chen Gong, "Latin America: Joint Efforts to Solve Debt Problem," *Beijing Review*, no. 27, July 2, 1984, p. 15.
28. "China Admitted to GATT Group," *Beijing Review*, no. 1, January 2, 1984, p. 11.
29. Liu Changqin and Yang Rongjia, "Economic Situation and Its Impact in African Countries," *Guoji Wenti Yanjiu* (Beijing), no. 1, January 1984, abridged translation in *Beijing Review*, no. 28, July 9, 1984, pp. 26–31.
30. Dan Lin and Zhang Zhuji, "Policies Promote Economic Growth," *Beijing Review*, no. 10, March 5, 1984, p. 15.

Chapter 7

CHINA'S SUPPORT FOR PEOPLE'S WAR IN THE 1980s

by Lillian Craig Harris

In his classic study *Autopsy on People's War,* Chalmers Johnson begins with the observation that his essay may be more a vivisection than an autopsy.[1] In the decade and more since publication of that study, people's war has still not died. It is no longer advocated in the context of world revolution, but it retained its qualities of both shibboleth and ideological weapon and has not been rejected by China either as a doctrine or as a foreign and domestic policy tool. People's war is a concept that appeals to the revolutionary spirit of many Chinese as well as to the institutional desire of the Chinese Communist Party to believe that Mao's revolutionary doctrine is internationally and eternally applicable. The doctrine is extremely useful politically, not least in the Third World, where the continued importance of people's war for China is illustrated by the fact that the Chinese are promoting the concept as a means to force Soviet compliance in two of the three situations cited by China as obstacles to normalization of Sino-Soviet relations: the Soviet occupation of Afghanistan and the Vietnamese occupation of Kampuchea.

The concept of people's war is woven into the warp and woof of the Chinese Communist experience and cannot but continue to color the world view of present Chinese leaders. Its roots go deep into the most seminal experiences of Chinese leadership for whom people's war—the experience of poorly equipped forces using

120

patience, guile, self-sacrifice, and unity to overcome larger more powerful forces—saved China. Thus people's war is central to the legitimacy of the Chinese Communist Party because it was central to the antinationalist and anti-Japanese conflicts which brought the CCP to power.

For many years after 1949, Beijing came close to being an international pariah, excluded from the United Nations and officially recognized by less than half of the world's nations. Application of people's war both domestically and abroad during that period was one critical way in which China "stood up." The concept helped to legitimize the new regime by providing a framework in which China's experience gained importance as part of a larger historical movement to extend communism outside China. Then as China's likely political isolation became evident to the new leadership, the concept became a means of thumbing a Chinese nose at the international rejection.

The symbolic content of the concept is of major importance. People's war is a playing out of the struggle motif that during various periods has occupied a primary position in Chinese Communist rhetoric. During the time of radical Maoism, hatred for China's enemies and for those who oppose the will of "the broad masses" was a virtue to be cultivated in opposition to the characteristics of passivity displayed by "Old China" under imperialism. In the 1960s, the Soviets could afford to compromise with imperialism and capitalism by calling for peaceful coexistence. But China was still caught in the dilemma of a search for international recognition. Although Beijing claimed that people's war did not exclude "peaceful coexistence" (the former was an internal matter; the latter dealt with relations between nations), China sought a revolutionary path to much desired international acceptance. It offered itself as a model and champion to Third World underdogs, preaching a doctrine that promised freedom from colonialism, fascism, neocolonialism, and imperialism.[2]

The post-Mao leadership seldom mentions "people's war," a term that has, in fact, become somewhat of an embarrassment to Beijing's new internationalism. Nonetheless, despite shifts in policy emphasis, people's war remains part of Chinese Communist doctrine. Whereas in the 1930s and 1940s the concept of people's war was the predominant strategy and united front tactics were simply a means to accomplish the end, today the united front concept has become the strategy. The concept of people's war is currently subordinated, regarded as a useful fringe tactic as long as it does not get in the way of major goals. Credit for laying "the foundation for establishing a new world order" is today given to the Five Principles of Peaceful Coexistence, not to people's war. But under the rubric "armed struggle" or even "just struggle," the concept continues to be applied selectively in various international situations. Moreover, with reference to Afghanistan and Kampuchea, "people's war" is still directly advocated.[3]

This Chinese switch to "internationalism" is rooted in China's need to take advantage of the economic and technological benefits of the developed world. The primacy of economics over ideology is a necessary component of the Four Modernizations. But the downplaying of people's war also reflects a changed world situation in which—of the four major evils of imperialism, colonialism, neocolonialism, and fascism that people's war is intended to combat—only imperialism (including Soviet "social imperialism") can still be defined as a major threat to the developing world. When it suits China's political purpose of identification with the Third World and reluctance to take sides in Third World conflict, regional efforts at self-aggrandizement such as those mounted by Libya and Iran are conveniently ignored. Where countering such hegemony suits China's purposes, as with South Africa and Israel, appropriate denunciations are made.

From its inception, the doctrine of people's war has been one of the most galvanizing revolutionary principles of the 20th century. Defense Minister Lin Biao's 1965 essay, "Long Live the Victory of People's War,"[4] appeared as the highwater mark of the doctrine. But the concept had been around at least since the 1930s, drawing its strength from the subsuming of the five basic theories of Chinese communism: the theory of contradiction, the united front concept, the centrality of armed struggle, the principle of self-reliance, and the idea of China as a model for revolution and development.

Broadly appealed to outside China—and sometimes applied in ways not those of Mao—people's war in its original form was a uniquely Chinese political tool. It called for mobilization of peasants as revolutionaries and held out the hope of victory to those engaged in hopeless causes. As defined by Lin, the concept of people's war foreshadows the Three Worlds Theory by calling for armed struggle pitting developing against developed countries in order to bring a halt to exploitation. In evident analogy to China's own revolutionary experience of mobilization of the peasant masses, Lin called for the encirclement of the world cities (the developed world) by the world's rural areas (the underdeveloped world).

The essence of the doctrine of people's war is that Communist cadre will mobilize and lead guerrilla wars which will eventually expand into regular warfare, leading to the replacement of unjust governments by mass-based (Communist) governments. In this process, conclusion of united fronts with other nationalist movements is both permitted and desirable. The precept that revolution cannot be exported is also central to the doctrine of people's war. People's war must be generated from within a country and in accordance with that country's internal conditions. Lin's article itself contained clear statements that China expected Vietnam to fight its own struggle and not to rely on Chinese intervention. Nonetheless, the article was widely regarded as a manual for international revolution.

People's War Lives

Although less important today as a strategic framework, people's war in the 1980s retains importance for shaping political concepts. It has both theoretical and practical applications and is useful in efforts to achieve the following goals:

- The most urgent and obvious use of people's war in the context of present Chinese foreign policy is to put *pressure on the Soviet Union* in those areas where China fears that the Soviet Union is extending its influence. Primarily they are Indochina and Afghanistan, but also include southern Africa and the Palestinian conflict with Israel. In the first two cases Chinese policy includes active involvement in the forms of military and economic aid and advice. The latter two situations are more complicated and appear to be largely motivated by a desire to show consistent support for popular Third World causes and to avoid leaving the field completely to the Soviets. The continued supply of limited amounts of arms is to ensure that Beijing retains at least some political clout with a variety of Palestinian and African groups.
- In the Third World continued adherence to the doctrine of

people's war allows China to *retain its revolutionary creden-tials* as a supporter of popular Third World causes such as Palestinian rights and the fight for freedom in Afghanistan.

- Where *colonialism* is still perceived to operate, as in southern Africa and Israel, China advocates people's war as *a legitimate counteraction*. However, a new pragmatism in advocacy of people's war allows armed struggle to be complemented by diplomatic activity and efforts to reach a negotiated solution. In such situations the objective appears to be use of "revolutionary struggle" *to keep the seriousness of the problem before the aggressor/exploiter so as eventually to force him to the bargaining table*.

- Domestically, people's war is part of the mental and ideological framework of the People's Liberation Army, and clear rejection of the doctrine would alienate Chinese military leaders, as it would many of their former comrades-in-arms now in government. But official use of the term is almost exclusively by military leaders who cite it—in a motherhood and apple pie sense—to *rally support for their positions* on any number of issues. Moreover, lip service is sometimes paid to the doctrine by political leaders in an effort to *manipulate the military leadership* with which the party hierarchy frequently finds itself in political conflict, pitting pragmatic modernizers against revolutionary veterans. Nonetheless, while the historical importance of the concept is played to, people's war has in fact been forced into the procrustean bed of modernization and its importance downgraded. However, "people's war" cuts two ways: If the military demands a greater share of modernization funding, it can be reminded of its glorious success in people's war—when as a peasant-based military force it had nothing—and told to make do with less. Nonetheless, the apparent Chinese government commitment to modern arms, an educated officer corps, and a more professional, less ideological military is a clear rejection of the Maoist concept of "people's war" as a central component of the Chinese experience.[5]

- Support for dissident Communist parties and insurrections in Southeast Asia—even though at an all time low—provides for China the *self-satisfaction of "not deserting old friends."* It also provides, of course, the *opportunity to increase pressure on regional governments* should that be deemed necessary.[6]

Metamorphosis of the Doctrine

The metamorphosis of people's war from a broad, active stage to a more theoretical and much highly selective stage coincided with the changing of the ideological guard at the end of the Cultural Revolution. One major reason for changes in the concept's application was purely pragmatic: It was unsuccessful outside China. In large measure the active promotion of people's war was an effort to persuade other countries to accept China's world view of the 1950s and 1960s. Many Third World countries reacted quite negatively to this intrusive Chinese philosophy, seeing in it both a danger to internal stability and a rejection of necessary relationships with the developed world. The fact that most other developing countries cannot be as self-reliant as China because they are so much smaller and have fewer resources contributed to resentment against China.

Chinese competition with the Soviet Union in the early 1960s to present an attractive model for revolution and development fell flat. Beijing's efforts to promote revolution in Africa led to ejection of Chinese diplomats and breaking of diplomatic ties with several African countries. In Latin America competition developed between the Chinese and Cuban revolutionary models despite Chinese statements in the late 1950s and early 1960s that the Cuban model was applicable in Latin America. Indonesian perception of a Chinese hand behind the abortive coup of 1965 resulted in a rupture of relations between the two states that has not yet been repaired.

These failures, attributed to the foreign policies of Liu Shaoqi, gave opportunity for application of more radical Maoist doctrine. In the second half of the 1960s, the Maoists argued that previous policy failures resulted from lack of reliance on Communist parties as the vanguard and commitment instead to united fronts with non-Communist groups, a situation which eventually resulted in the coming to power of anti-Communist governments. The answer provided by the Maoists was sponsorship of Communist insurgencies and pro-Chinese splinter groups wherever possible. Unfortunately from the Maoists' viewpoint, revolutionary foreign policy with its central ingredient of people's war failed to create any new Communist states or even any strong pro-Chinese Communist parties. Instead, the Communist world was factionalized and China further ostracized even by many Third World countries.

Following admission to the United Nations in 1971, China began to reestablish and expand diplomatic and trade ties soured or broken by Cultural Revolution tactics. After the violent 1960s decade, the policy of support for people's war was reconsidered and amended. This decision was part of a general deemphasis of the value of armed revolution and a pullback from an aggressive international stance that had led to isolation and hostility to one promoting peaceful coexistence and interaction. Over a period of time, several of the liberation and "revolutionary" causes (such as the rebellion in Oman's Dhofar Province) China had previously supported were abandoned. Beginning in the mid-1970s, Chinese support for oppositionist Communist parties, especially in Southeast Asia, sharply diminished.

Meanwhile, although the doctrine of people's war itself has not been officially redefined, its application has been considerably amended—and limited. In Afghanistan, for example, non-Communist cadre engage in it with Chinese encouragement against Communist cadre. Moreover, in the early 1970s China, deciding to take a more pragmatic line in keeping with its own national interests, took a closer look at the idea of "the people" as any group opposing authority. Thus, there was no Chinese support for people's war by the Muslim people who sought to establish Bangladesh in 1971, a failure that led to considerable finger pointing at China by Third World "revolutionaries."

Since 1978 the Three Worlds Theory has been deemphasized, although not formally renounced, and since the Twelfth Party Congress in 1982, China has declared a return to the politics of the Bandung era which underscores the need for peaceful coexistence. China's post-1982 "independent" foreign policy results from the desire to secure for China a position of recognized significance, regional and global leadership, and security—concepts in obvious contradiction to a doctrine proclaiming the need to change other governments through violent means.

A Pragmatic Approach to Support for Third World Conflicts

People's war is today most notable for where China does not apply it. Throughout the world there are a variety of ready-made conflicts whose participants, in an earlier era, would have received rhetorical and probably at least limited military support from China. Yet in the mid-1980s, Chinese support for revolutionary armed struggle is surprisingly infrequent. If a conflict has general Third World recognition as a legitimate popular war against tyranny and injustice, China usually gives verbal support. But Beijing seldom provides direct assistance. Included among the situations where Chinese support for armed struggle is most noticeably lacking are Central America, Chad, Lebanon, Sudan, and the Western Sahara. All these situations include the basic ingredients for people's war:

- People who will organize and fight, the "revolutionary vanguard."
- Space/land in which partisans can be found and operations carried out.
- A guiding ideology centering on national identity and aimed at self-determination and self-government.

Certainly, a part of China's reluctance stems from the desire to avoid taking sides in other countries' complex domestic quarrels, thus risking coming out on the losing side and damaging state-to-state relations, as the Chinese did in Angola in the early 1970s. China also has learned to its bitter experience that not every rebellion is capable of growing into a full-fledged revolution. Support for a variety of fringe groups in Africa and Latin America in the 1960s served no ultimate purpose other than to gain for China a reputation in some Third World circles as an international meddler. Then, too, post-Mao China has radically altered financial and political priorities. But the real key to this failure of support is an embarrassing one: China has no theoretical means to discuss world "hot spots" which are not attributable to superpower hegemony but rather to conflict between Third World countries themselves. Simply put, where the situation is not anti-imperialist, people's war cannot be applied.

In the mid-1980s, where China decides that it cannot or should not support armed conflict, it tends to describe the situation as a civil conflict and to stress the need for all outside interference to cease. For example, in the case of the Moroccan claim to the Western Sahara, there is no Third World consensus on which side is right. Nor is there a non-Third World aggressor. For China to support the Polisario would be to side with majority Third World opinion but would alienate China from Morocco, a valued Third

World friend. With regard to civil conflict in Sudan, for China to assist John Garang and the Sudanese People's Liberation Army, or any other southern Sudanese group fighting against domination by northern, Arabized Sudanese, would involve the Chinese in a legitimate contest for "national independence," but risk contributing to regional disunity and destabilization from which the Soviet Union would seek to benefit. It would also traumatize China's ties with a major African country and have negative repercussions on China's ties with the Arab world in general.

Lebanon presents China with an even more difficult problem. In the early years of the Lebanese conflict (1975–1977), Beijing focused little attention on that country's difficulties. Embarrassed by growing Palestinian and Syrian involvement, China could not choose between friends and instead characterized the Lebanese chaos as a religious conflict. Eventual Israeli and then U.S. involvement provided China with scapegoats acceptable to the Third World. But still, although China would almost certainly have given at least verbal support to some Lebanese faction or factions in the 1960s, Beijing has avoided direct involvement, calling instead for an indigenous Lebanese solution and a halt to all foreign intervention so as to avoid giving opportunity to the Soviets.

What appears to be more significant to direct Chinese involvement than the characteristics of the individual situation is the common lack of one major ingredient: direct involvement by either the Soviet Union or the United States. Although China clearly believes that the Soviet Union is a greater threat to world peace than is the United States, China's efforts to "balance" its foreign policy imply that China must support opposition to U.S. hegemony if China is to support indigenous efforts against Soviet hegemony. Certainly since 1982 the Chinese definition of hegemony has included political interference, as well as military intervention, in other countries' affairs. Thus, Chinese support for political/military struggles in South Africa and Palestine—and perhaps even more graphically in Central America—are at least in part motivated by desire to counter U.S. as well as Soviet policy.

In South Africa, where there is only peripheral Soviet involvement, Chinese support appears motivated by desire to guard against any increase in Soviet influence in Africa (while staying on the correct side of a popular Third World cause). The situation provides opportunity to take the moral high road in criticism of U.S. policy. In Central America, also described by China as a world "hot spot," instability provides high risk of increased Soviet and U.S. influence. With regard to Nicaragua and El Salvador, China supports regional efforts toward a peaceful political solution, such as those sponsored by the Contadora Group, but warns Washington against letting Moscow increase its influence in the U.S. backyard.

But perhaps China's treatment of the Libyan invasion of Chad presents most clearly the pragmatic nature of China's present policy on support for popular struggle. Here is no First or Second World colonial power laying claim to a developing Third World country, but a large Third World "revolutionary" state—armed by the Soviet Union—pursuing its irredentist claims at the expense of a weaker neighbor. By all rights China should support that weak neighbor in its opposition to Libyan occupation. Yet although on at least one occasion in 1981 the Chinese media took Libya to task for its invasion of Chad, China has provided no support to the Chadian government or to any other Chadian group.

Nor has this clear case of Third World colonialism precipitated any change in China's relations with Libya. The Chinese appear to take the view that although Qadhafi's destabilizing activities provide opportunity to the Soviets, because Qadhafi himself remains wary of Moscow, he is not likely to fall under Soviet influence. Beijing seeks, therefore, to stay on good terms with the Libyan leader as a significant Third World figure. In presenting his credentials to Qadhafi in March 1985, the new Chinese ambassador expressed his great joy in "representing my country to this brave people which leads the struggle against imperialism and colonization in all forms."[7]

Modern Applications of People's War

Where China today actively supports armed struggle, there is either active Soviet involvement or the Chinese find themselves seeking to retain influence with dissidents or rebels so as to avoid leaving the field to the Soviets. This principle holds true for China's support for armed struggle in Afghanistan and Kampuchea as well as its support for the Palestinians and for efforts by blacks to fight white supremacy in southern Africa.

Southeast Asia. The sole exception is Chinese support—albeit at much reduced levels—for opposition Communist parties in

Southeast Asia. Although China denies it provides aid, it continues to give party-to-party backing and probably at least some material support to the Burma Communist Party (BCP) and to the Malaysian Communist Party, both of which are engaged in military action against legitimate governments. (There were indications, including cessation of "Voice of the People of Burma" radio broadcasts from southern China in early 1985, that China had stopped material support to the BCP as a prelude to a visit to China by Burmese leader Ne Win in May. Such cutoffs have previously occurred, however, but not lasted.) China also maintains contacts with the Thai People's Liberation Armed Forces, the Communist Party of Indonesia (PKI), and—according to some unconfirmed reports—with the Communist Party of the Philippines, to all of which it has provided people's war support and encouragement in years past.

Although China appears committed to retaining traditional ties with regional Communist parties, since the end of the Cultural Revolution it has significantly reduced its contacts with Communist groups involved in Southeast Asian insurgencies. In an early 1981 press conference in Bangkok, Chinese Premier Zhao Ziyang declared that China would maintain ties with Southeast Asian Communist-led insurgencies but hoped as well to cultivate closer ties to regional governments. Elsewhere, Zhao described China's support for Communist parties in ASEAN countries as "mainly political and moral" and repeated China's disapproval of the export of revolution and interference in other countries' internal affairs.

Chinese motivation for continued support appears to be the wish to avoid the appearance of deserting old friends (as Beijing has described it), while maintaining a lever to use as necessary to remind local governments of China's importance in regional politics. Continued contacts with these fringe groups, in particular the Thai Communists, are also intended by China to prevent a turning to the Vietnamese Communist Party. The special importance to China of the Asian Third World due to proximity and historical ties makes the case of Chinese support for Southeast Asian Communist parties a peculiar exception in China's modern application of the doctrine of people's war.

Indochina. The basic Chinese motivation in supporting Khmer resistance to Vietnamese aggression is to counter the expansion of Soviet influence on China's borders. Secondarily, Beijing wishes to assert to Vietnam China's right to regional primacy. Ironically, the deterioration of China's previously close ties with North Vietnam after Hanoi's victory over South Vietnam isolated the SRV and gave it little alternative to closer ties with the Soviet Union. The contribution of people's war to victory in Vietnam, achieved in part with Chinese support, led to an at least nominally unified Vietnam with a desire for regional influence and a marked distaste for China's unspoken but evident claims to regional leadership.

The regional balance of power shifted following the 1978 Vietnamese invasion of Kampuchea, aligning China with Thailand and resulting in extensive Chinese support for both Communist and non-Communist Khmer resistance groups. China has sought by use of military means (the 1979 border war to "teach Vietnam a lesson") and political pressuring (advocating punitive international economic and political measures against Vietnam) to counter Vietnamese regional self-aggrandizement. Neither of these avenues has had a significant impact on Vietnamese intentions, and since 1980 China has become ever more deeply involved in support for guerrilla warfare to achieve Kampuchea's national liberation.

The full extent of Chinese aid to the Khmer resistance is not known. However, China admits that it supports "the Kampuchean people's war against the Vietnamese aggressors" and has supplied large quantities of arms, food, and other supplies as well as financial support for the Kampuchean fighters. In early 1985 it appeared that Chinese military advisers with logistical and support role functions might be supplied to the resistance forces. If these advisers should eventually find themselves involved in combat, self-reliance, a major tenet of people's war, would clearly have been violated.

China is aware of ASEAN sensitivities to its support for the discredited Khmer Rouge group and has sought to balance its role by increasing aid to non-Communist resistance groups. In January 1985, Chinese Foreign Minister Wu Xueqian announced that China would increase aid to Son Sann's Khmer People's National Liberation Front, one of two non-Communist factions of the Democratic Kampuchean coalition led by Prince Norodom Sihanouk. Meanwhile, China has consistently resisted calls for an international conference on Kampuchea, stressing instead the need for resistance, unity, and persistence in a protracted struggle along classic people's war lines. In 1985, as the Khmer resistance suffered severe setbacks at the hands of Vietnamese forces, China advised the Khmer to regroup in small, mobile strike units rather than continue to rely on static defenses.[8]

China also has engaged in consistent efforts to persuade ASEAN and the United States to become more involved in the anti-Vietnamese struggle on the grounds that Vietnam is serving as a Soviet surrogate. Although China itself has issued frequent threats to "teach Vietnam a second lesson," it actually has limited options to do so and is not likely once again to commit its forces to a border war in an effort to draw Vietnamese troops out of Kampuchea. Instead, continuation of people's war is the preferred option.

Afghanistan.   Chinese involvement in Afghan resistance to Soviet occupation is less extensive due both to logistics and distance. Nonetheless, Afghanistan is a Chinese border state whose 1979 invasion by the Soviet army was described by China as a direct threat to Chinese national security. Beijing continues to give propaganda and materiel support to "the Afghan people's war against Soviet aggression." As in the case of Kampuchea, the Chinese objective in promoting people's war in Afghanistan is defensive: a halt to advance by the Soviet Union or one of its surrogates on the Chinese border and relief from the pressures of Soviet "encirclement" of China.

China'a ability to supply the Afghan *mujahidin* with light, portable weapons suitable to guerrilla warfare, weapons whose parts and ammunition are often interchangeable with captured Soviet weapons, has been particularly helpful to the resistance. In March 1985 Radio Kabul charged that since 1980 China had supplied $400 million in weapons, including surface-to-air missiles, to the resistance groups. The official Afghan radio also claimed that China had begun to supply the resistance directly as well as through Pakistan and said the Chinese were operating four guerrilla training centers in Pakistan. Actually, Pakistani sensitivities have probably prevented involvement of Chinese military advisers, whose presence may not in any case be necessary given the Afghans' long competence in guerrilla warfare.

China has played a major role in keeping Soviet activities in Afghanistan before international attention—a prime objective of people's war. However, in late 1984 Chinese efforts to improve ties with the Soviet Union caused Beijing to lower the volume of its rhetoric against Soviet involvement in Afghanistan. In December 1984 on the fifth anniversary of the Soviet invasion, China for the first time failed to issue a statement condemning the event.

Nonetheless, Chinese determination to resist Soviet advance through promotion of Afghan armed struggle has not diminished. Public statements and diplomatic protest by the Afghan government in early 1985 indicate that Chinese aid may actually have increased. Beijing has countered as "slander" Kabul's charges that China is maintaining a training camp for *mujahidin* in Xinjiang and that China serves as the main center for organization of Afghan resistance.

With Afghanistan as with Kampuchea, China appears committed to continued encouragement for a course of people's war rather than negotiated settlement. Beijing rebuffed a January 1985 offer by the People's Democratic Party of Afghanistan (PDPA) to establish party-to-party ties in exchange for an end to Chinese aid to the Afghan resistance. The PDPA then issued a letter comparing Soviet military support for Afghanistan to Soviet support to the CCP in 1945. But the Chinese remained unimpressed.

Palestine. Since formation of the Palestine Liberation Organization in 1964, China has been a supporter of Palestinian armed struggle. Before the Soviet Union became actively involved with the Palestinians in 1969, China had a virtual monopoly on arms supplies to the various Palestinian guerrilla groups. Of the multitude of Palestinian groups, Fatah has received the largest share of Chinese aid due to Beijing's perception that Fatah stood the greatest chance of uniting the Palestinian people. Yasir Arafat continues to visit China periodically.

In the late 1960s, China frequently called for the extermination of Israel and appeared to believe that the Palestinians represented a vanguard for eventual liberation of the Arab world from both "neocolonialism" and the corruption and oppression of the Arab regimes themselves. But the near total rout of Palestinian guerrillas by the Jordanian army in Black September 1970—which coincided with the beginning of China's own reappraisal of foreign policy—cured China of its Palestinian leadership delusions.[9]

Since 1970, China's support for various Palestinian groups has continued but has gradually moved from a philosophy of support for active people's war to admonitions to seek a negotiated settlement. Low levels of arms supply continue, but Chinese rhetoric has moved from emphasis on Palestinian "armed struggle" to support for the Palestinians' "just struggle." A major Chinese objective in supporting the Palestinian guerrillas is to avoid leaving these groups solely to Soviet influence. Furthermore, the Chinese are also aware that nonsupport for "the Arab cause" would have negative political reverberations not only in the Arab world, but in the Third World generally.

Nonetheless, because Beijing recognizes that regional stability would close a major arms market to the Soviets and thus deprive Moscow of a prime means of political and economic access, Palestinian operations into Israel have been increasingly ignored or downplayed by Chinese media in recent years. However, China has consistently, through public statements and UN resolutions, emphasized its view that "the Palestinian issue is the crux of the Middle East question" and that restoration of Palestinian rights, including Israeli withdrawal from all Arab territory occupied since 1967, is essential for regional peace. But China now recognizes the validity of Israel's existence as a state and has been sharply criticized in some Arab circles for taking a positive outlook on the Egypt-Israel peace treaty.

The complexity of the Arab-Israeli conflict—with possibilities for damage to China's Third World credentials—has been increased by recent conclusion of Chinese arms deals with Israel. Arms agreements are denied by both parties but appear to include Israeli reequipping of Chinese tanks with modern guns and fire control systems as well as the sale to China of antiship missiles.[10]

Through the years China's relations with the Palestinian groups have sometimes been complicated by the issue of international terrorism. Despite support for people's war, China has never supported terrorist actions such as hijacking, which it regards as a contradiction of true revolutionary principles. Nonetheless, the Chinese draw a distinction between guerrilla actions in occupied territory and international terrorism. Thus, while Palestinian assaults on civilian targets in Israeli-occupied territory might not be deemed wise by China, such activity is ideologically acceptable as in keeping with the rules of people's war. On the other hand, China regards Israeli activities in Lebanon as a form of government-sponsored terrorism and comes close to endorsing the view espoused by Libya's Qadhafi that U.S. support for Israel is itself an act of international terrorism.

Southern Africa. In pre-independence Angola China supported the National Union for the Total Independence of Angola (UNITA), and before Rhodesia became Zimbabwe, Beijing provided major support to Robert Mugabe's Zimbabwe African National Union (ZANU). Desire to avoid the errors of the 1960s continues to infuse Chinese aid to African insurgent groups with a tone of caution. Since the 1960s, China has probably not involved itself in any covert efforts to overthrow black African governments.

The gradual elimination of colonialism from Africa has narrowed the scope for people's war on that continent. But China maintains ties with several liberation groups in southern Africa to which it donates limited amounts of arms and liberal amounts of political support. These include the South-West Africa People's Organization (SWAPO) in Namibia and both the Pan-Africanist Congress and the African National Congress. China is frustrated by factionalism among these groups, and so a major thrust of Chinese advice to the latter two is that they unite their efforts against South Africa.

The Chinese, who take the position that "the racist rule of the South African authorities [is] the root cause of the unrest and turmoil in southern Africa," appear committed to a policy of support for insurgent groups despite parallel support for a negotiated solution. Essentially, China supports the black African position which encourages both military and political pressure. And China supports as well the black African position that the way to force South Africa to compliance is through international isolation.

It is doubtful that China expects armed struggle to do more in southern Africa than apply limited additional pressure. Nonetheless, Chinese support for African liberation causes is highly popular in the Third World. Through involvement in southern African insurgencies, the Chinese also hope to counter the rise of Soviet influence over these movements and thus over the governments their leaders will eventually form. SWAPO leader Sam Nujoma visited China in 1983, after which Chinese aid to the PAC/ANC has increased.

Conclusion

There is no question that China continues to find the doctrine of people's war a useful policy tool both at home and abroad. It is also clear that the doctrine remains politically sensitive and controversial even within the Chinese hierarchy. Clearly, some in the leadership coalition regard people's war as a piece of Maoist baggage that must eventually be rejected. Present efforts to "weed out the elements of left-wing radicalism in the army" certainly include removal of those who advocate people's war in its more pure form. Using fire to fight fire, the moderate leadership now holds up the 1935 Zunyi Conference (where Mao's leftist ideology first gained precedence as the dominant party line) as the model of

central party control over the military. Continued support for
Asian Communist parties whose policy is to advance people's war
is probably, at least in part, a result of compromise by moderate
Chinese leaders with those of a more militant, Maoist persuasion.

Given this controversy, as well as the usefulness of people's war
in selected situations, it is doubtful that China will officially
renounce the doctrine of people's war in the foreseeable future.
Under the general rubric of support for armed struggle against
Soviet advance, the doctrine will remain alive and well at least in
Indochina and Afghanistan for sometime to come. But it will most
likely continue to be downplayed in the Middle East and Africa in
favor of negotiated peace settlements, as it has been in Southeast
Asia in favor of better relations with regional governments.

However, Chinese failure to renounce the doctrine will continue
to have negative repercussions on China's Third World relationships, particularly with China's Asian neighbors. Southeast Asians
recognize that

> *periods of Communist and chauvinist Chinese militancy have alter-*
> *nated with periods of "peaceful coexistence". . . (and) assume,*
> *rightly or wrongly, that the CCP views the Communist parties of*
> *Southeast Asia as potential weapons against their national govern-*
> *ments if the latter became antagonistic to Chinese interests.*[11]

Chinese encouragement for people's war against Vietnam rein-
forces this perception regardless of how the Southeast Asian
nations feel about Vietnamese aggression.

Suspicions of Chinese intentions in other parts of the Third
World—Africa in particular—due to China's past support for people's war there have largely been overcome by subsequent aid
programs and correct behavior. But there are lingering fears that
China could some day turn again to radical behavior. These fears
are fed by China's continued failure to become actively involved in
major Third World organizations such as the Non-Aligned Movement and the Group of 77. But China also faces a credibility gap in
the Third World due, at least in part, to refusal to renounce the use
of force either for solution of domestic problems or in international
affairs. Although the Chinese have gone to considerable lengths to
stress peaceful intentions toward Hong Kong and Taiwan in the
"reunification" process, there are those who point to Beijing's
unwillingness to renounce the use of force if necessary to effect
political change as evidence of Chinese untrustworthiness.

Finally, although many Third World states believe China offers useful advice on distancing from superpower politics and helpful support for Third World positions, there is a parallel perception that China is not actually a Third World country but a nascent great power whose future course remains uncertain.[12] China is unlikely to turn again to the radical politics of the 1960s. But promotion of surrogate wars, no matter the justice of the cause, does nothing to retard the international perception that it might.

Endnotes

1. Chalmers Johnson, *Autopsy on People's War* (Berkeley: University of California Press, 1973).
2. Peter Van Ness, in *Revolution and Chinese Foreign Policy: Peking's Support for Wars of National Liberation* (Berkeley: University of California Press, 1970), provides a detailed and fascinating analysis of the application of people's war during the 1960s.
3. For an overview of the evolution of China's policy toward and relations with the Third World, see Lillian Craig Harris, *China's Foreign Policy Toward the Third World* (Washington, D.C.: The Center for Strategic and International Studies, Georgetown University, *Washington Papers*, No. 112, 1985).
4. Lin Biao, *Long Live the Victory of People's War* (Beijing: Foreign Languages Press, 1965).
5. See, for example, Daniel Southerland, "China Seeks More Professional Army," *Washington Post*, June 5, 1985, p. A–28.
6. Conflict in the Third World—be it people's war or not—is also potentially useful to China in one other more cynical manner. China faces an acute dilemma that pits its financial needs for the hard currency available through international arms sales against its recognition that continued instability enhances Soviet opportunism. China is now publicly acknowledged to have sold large quantities of arms to both Iran and Iraq, although the Chinese government hotly denies that it is involved in selling arms to either and calls publicly for a negotiated settlement of the war. Nonetheless, China's earnings from arms sales to the Middle East alone totaled, according to some estimates, $5 billion from 1982 to 1984. See, for example, "China: Birth of an Arms Salesman," *The Economist* (London), November 17, 1984, p. 40. It is unclear how much of this alleged amount has been delivered and paid for.
7. Tripoli JANA, March 9, 1985, in Foreign Broadcast Information Service, *Daily Report: Middle East and North Africa*, March 11, 1985, p. Q1.
8. "Clean Sweep: The Last Khmer Base Falls," *Time*, March 25, 1985, p. 29.
9. An explanation of the evolution of Chinese policy toward the Palestinian organizations in the late 1960s is found in Yitzhak Shichor, *The Middle East in China's Foreign Policy: 1949–1977* (Cambridge: Cambridge University Press, 1979).
10. "Israeli-PRC Military Collaboration Reported," *Sunday Times* (London), October 14, 1984, p. 23.

11. Guy J. Pauker, "Southeast Asia Looks at China," in Harrison Brown (editor), *China Among the Nations of the Pacific* (Boulder, Co.: Westview Press, 1982), p. 121.

12. A persuasive discussion of the problems China faces in its efforts to identify with the Third World is found in Harry Harding, "China and the Third World: From Revolution to Containment," in Richard H. Solomon (editor), *The China Factor: Sino-American Relations and the Global Scene* (Englewood Cliffs, N.J.: Prentice-Hall, Inc., 1981).

Chapter 8

THE THIRD WORLD LOOKS AT CHINA

by Robert A. Manning

The old Washington adage that where you stand depends on where you sit is instructive for understanding both Chinese foreign policy toward the Third World and Third World perceptions of it. As both an emerging world power and a developing country, China has a unique global role. It is at once a nuclear power, a major factor in the great power triangle (the United States, the Soviet Union, China) and a resource-rich less-developed nation.

In terms of practical consequence, however, China's security interests, political interests, and military force projection capabilities become increasingly symbolic the farther one gets from its Asian borders. China's economic interests are more global in character and its economic concerns are more North-South and South-South in nature than they are regionally-oriented. In general, Chinese foreign policy toward the Third World is not a regional policy. Rather, it is guided by universal concepts: the Five Principles of Peaceful Coexistence, a global anti-Sovietism, an adherence to the goals of the nonaligned movement (that is, anti-colonialism, independence from the superpowers, call for a new international economic order), and in recent years, an emphasis on South-South cooperation.

While the precepts of Chinese policy toward the Third World have not changed dramatically, there have been important tactical and strategic policy shifts in the post-Mao period. There has been in practice, if not in theory, a deemphasis on supporting revolutionary guerrilla groups, a move away from knee-jerk anti-Sovietism and toward a more genuinely nonaligned approach to dealing with Third World countries. This is most dramatically evidenced by China's dwindling support for Marxist insurgents in Asia and by the normalization of relations with two key Soviet allies, Cuba and Angola. This more normative approach to its foreign policy reflects Beijing's growing integration into the world political and economic system and has resulted increasingly in the Third World perception of China more as a status quo, albeit developing nation, power.

This shift in the orientation of Chinese foreign policy in the post-Mao period led to new and still evolving Third World views of China. Beijing's downgrading of the anti-Soviet thrust in its foreign policy and general abandoning of support for insurgent national liberation movements has made China appear less menacing to Third World regimes, particularly in Africa and Asia. China's role as an actor in the global institutionalized framework has been welcomed as providing a much needed impetus to the Third World political and economic agenda in the context of the Non-Aligned Movement and North-South issues. The downside of China's behavior as an increasingly status quo power is that it is viewed as an emerging great power whose interests may not always coincide with the small nations and mini-states of the Third World. This view of China as a great power tends to vary by region, looming larger, depending largely on geographic proximity to China.

The reaction to the broad change in China's economic policies has been mixed. Beijing's success in development and its hybrid version of market socialism is increasingly looked to as a model by many less-developed countries. But many newly industrializing countries have begun to view China more as a competitor for both global markets and for international capital flows. These fears of China's negative impact, both political and economic, are most pronounced in the nations on China's periphery.

Southeast Asia

China perceives itself as an independent actor, a peaceful nonaligned developing nation. Its less-developed Asian neighbors,

however, view China more as a stirring giant. This is particularly
true in Southeast Asia, where there is substantial scepticism, if not
outright hostility, toward the idea that a strong, modernized China
allied with the United States and Japan would be a benign actor.
There are several factors behind such scepticism toward China.
One key element is the role of overseas ethnic Chinese in the
national political and economic life of most ASEAN countries.
Another factor is the memory of past—and residual—Chinese
support for Communist parties in Malaysia, Indonesia, Thailand,
and Burma. A third source of tension is the growing fear among
ASEAN nations that China is increasingly becoming an economic
competitor.

Malaysia and Indonesia

Caution in regard to China and fear of its potential as a dominant
regional power is particularly acute in Malaysia, where overseas
Chinese comprise 36 percent of the population, and in Indonesia
with some four million Chinese. In both cases, the overseas
Chinese play a disproportionately large economic and social role.
A leading Indonesian paper commented, "Washington is trying
hard to reconcile nations in East and Southeast Asia on the one
hand and the PRC on the other." The paper added that the U.S.
"policy of pampering the PRC" may turn "East and Southeast Asia
into a PRC sphere of influence."[1]

Nonetheless, Indonesia gradually increased its indirect trade
with China, which totaled some $300 million in 1983 (largely via
Singapore and Hong Kong). It was not until 1985, in the aftermath
of high-level talks between Chinese and Indonesian officials during
the 30th anniversary of the Bandung meeting (from which grew
the Non-Aligned Movement), that Sino-Indonesian direct trade
ties were reestablished amidst much controversy in Indonesia.
Similarly, Malaysia, with equal reticence, has gradually increased
trade and contact with China.

While both nations encourage economic integration with China,
they are also wary of Beijing. "The cautious posture that Indonesian leaders have been adopting towards China's eagerness to
increase Sino-Indonesian ties," said a Malaysian radio commentary, "is well appreciated by Malaysia. China has yet to come up
with a categorical statement that it will not interfere in the internal

affairs of Southeast Asian nations by supporting communist guerrillas."[2] Until the mid-1980s, Chinese language publications were
prohibited in Indonesia, underscoring the deeply ingrained cultural phobia. The ostensible obstacle blocking normalization of
relations is the Chinese unwillingness to meet Jakarta's demand
that it apologize for its role in the aborted 1965 Communist-led
coup attempt and admit its mistake. China has said that it only
maintains "moral relations" with Communist parties in the region
and has closed down some clandestine radio stations inside China
from which several Communist parties (from Thailand, Malaysia,
and Burma) had broadcast into their respective countries.

Indochina

It is in regard to Indochina, however, that the most cogent
example of the *realpolitik* character of Beijing's foreign policy
emerges. Sino-Vietnamese antagonism is a microcosm of Chinese
anti-Sovietism and nationalist rivalry for influence in the region.
There is also a particular historical rivalry played out in Chinese
efforts to undermine Vietnam's dominant role in Indochina. Officially, China supports the tripartite coalition of the Khmer Rouge,
Prince Sihanouk, and Son Sann. In practice, China has been the
chief backer of the infamous Khmer Rouge, which is the largest,
best equipped of the three and has done the overwhelming
majority of the fighting. A typical Vietnamese view of China's role
is embodied in an editorial in the official *Nhan Dan:*

> The reactionaries in Beijing ruling circles have intensified their
> provocative acts and land-grabbing attacks at the Sino-Vietnamese
> and Sino-Lao borders, encouraged Thai reactionaries to encroach
> upon Lao territory, and nurtured the genocidal Pol Pot remnants
> hiding in Thailand against the revival of the Kampuchean people.[3]

Ironically, China's active support for the Khmer Rouge has little
relationship to either Marxist ideology or a commitment to national
liberation movements. Rather, it is classic power politics seeking to
"bleed Vietnam" (and also drain Soviet resources), deterring Hanoi's efforts to be the dominant force on the Indochina peninsula.
The Kampuchea conflict also serves to create at least a short-term
set of common interests between ASEAN and China, which in the
absence of Vietnamese force in Kampuchea might not otherwise
exist. Thailand, a key frontline state in the conflict, has been drawn

closer to China as a guarantor against conflict with Vietnam. But there is a growing, though still largely subsurface, backlash against Chinese courting of prominent Thais and overseas Chinese-Thais, which may cast a pall over Sino-Thai relations when the Kampuchea conflict is resolved. Despite ASEAN opposition to the Vietnamese invasion of Kampuchea, many ASEAN states, particularly Malaysia and Indonesia, would like to see Vietnam distance itself from the Soviets and, after withdrawing its troops from Kampuchea upon gaining a settlement of the conflict, gradually bring Hanoi into the ASEAN fold as a counterweight to Chinese influence in Southeast Asia in the long term.[4]

Philippines

The Philippines is another Southeast Asian illustration of how national interest and anti-Sovietism prevail over ideology in Chinese foreign policy. Site of the two largest U.S. overseas bases— Subic Bay Naval Station and Clark Air Force Base—the Philippines is a key historic client of the United States in the region. The government is besieged by Maoist-oriented guerrillas of the Communist Party of the Philippines, and its armed wing, the New People's Army (CPP/NPA), is now active in at least 62 of the 73 provinces.

Fearing that instability in the post-Marcos era could lead to the ejection of U.S. bases and a diminution of the U.S. presence in the region, Beijing has assiduously ignored the CPP/NPA and made numerous gestures to support the Marcos regime. On the occasion of the tenth anniversary of normalized relations, the Chinese media carried numerous interviews of top Filipino officials and feted Marcos' son in Beijing. China has also supplied low-interest deferred payment loans to finance emergency rice shipments and petroleum to Manila, and signed a $500 million annual trade accord with the Marcos regime as well.

Such gestures were not lost on the Marcos government. Prime Minister Cesar Virata described Sino-Philippines relations as "very good." During an April 1985 visit, First Lady Imelda Marcos thanked Chinese Foreign Minister Wu Xueqian for China's noninterference in the Philippines internal affairs. The *Times-Journal* of Manila described the establishment of ties with China "a milestone in the history of Philippines foreign policy" and added, "our relations with China have been most beneficial."[5]

Northeast Asia

The Koreas

The Korean Peninsula is another key border area for China, underscored by the fact that North Korea is the only nation with whom Beijing has a bilateral security pact. But in this region as well, Chinese policy is marked by a businesslike pragmatism, which has been reciprocated by both North and South Korea. For North Korea, one of the most isolated nations in the world, China has been not only a guarantor of security, but also one of its few windows on and diplomatic conduits to the outside world. North Korea has sought, with considerable success, to play off China against its other key ally, the Soviet Union.

A remarkable development in the post-Mao period has been burgeoning Chinese ties with South Korea. Though Beijing has backed North Korean call for tripartite talks (United States, South Korea, and North Korea) on the reunification of Korea, it has played an active mediating role along with Japan and the United States in the negotiating process. South Korea views China as both an important interlocutor and restraining influence on North Korea and has actively sought to expand contacts with South Korea.

Though normalization is still a long way off, South Korea has rapidly expanded economic ties with China. For Seoul, China is a potentially important market in an increasingly competitive world, while for China, trade with South Korea is an element in its modernization strategy of intergrating the Chinese economy with the rest of East Asia. Chinese trade with South Korea is estimated to have reached some $800 million in 1984, much of it via Hong Kong. But Chinese and South Korean merchant ships have been docking in each other's ports, South Korean businessmen are increasingly visiting China, and moves toward direct Korean investment in China's New Economic Zones have been made.[6]

Moreover, since 1983 sports, cultural, and diplomatic contacts have increased. Sports exchanges between South Korea and China have, in fact, become routine. Moreover, South Korean diplomats have attended international conferences in Beijing, and the two countries have begun direct phone and postal links and tourism. In an August 1985 message to Chinese leaders, South Korean President Chun Doo Hwan urged expanding exchanges with China.

Taiwan

Though more complex due to mutual claims of sovereignty, China's ties with Taiwan have followed a similar course. China-Taiwan two-way trade mushroomed to some $550 million in 1984, and rose again to $500 million in the first five months of 1985, with total trade for the year projected to reach $1 billion. A leading Taiwan businessman said, "In Taiwan 99 percent of the businessmen think we should just trade and not talk about military and political affairs. Trade is the best way to lower tension."[7] However, for Taiwan, contacts with China have been primarily economic, and officially Taipei has resisted political overtures from China.

China's formulation of "one country, two systems," devised during successful talks with Britain to extend China's sovereignty to Hong Kong, is clearly aimed at Taiwan as well. China has sought to use economic contacts to expand overall ties. Taiwan businessmen have made secret trips to Fujian province across the Taiwan Strait as Beijing has sought to lure investment, and even has set up a special Taiwan affairs office in the province. While such developments underscore Beijing's pragmatism and willingness to separate business and politics, clearly there has been little concrete movement toward "peaceful reunification" with Taiwan. Both Taipei and Beijing continue to battle for the hearts and minds of the overseas Chinese. Increased contacts, particularly the large volume of trade, have set in motion forces softening Taipei's hostility toward Beijing. But there is little prospect of serious discussion on reunification until well after the Hong Kong accord is tested.

South Asia

South Asia, a lower priority for China than other areas on its perimeter, is illustrative of Beijing's modulated anti-Sovietism, realism, and increasing competitiveness with other developing countries. In the geopolitics of the region, Beijing has been closely allied with Pakistan and has strongly backed the Afghan rebels resisting the Soviet invasion of Afghanistan, in tandem with Pakistan and the United States. Not surprisingly, in geopolitical and economic terms India's view of Chinese policy is one of caution and wariness. In the 1980s India and China have moved toward easing tensions over border disputes and gravitated toward a de facto regional détente, though there is still an undercurrent of Indian scepticism stemming from Chinese support, particularly nuclear cooperation, with Pakistan. There is also a growing resentment due to the hard reality that India is China's major competitor as an emerging regional power, and that while Beijing is courted by the West, India is often taken for granted.

Perhaps the most profound and long-term source of Indian septicism about China is the growing element of economic competition. Though India has a more developed scientific and technical infrastructure, China has made rapid strides in these areas. Beijing is successfully competing with India for Third World markets in textiles, light manufacturing, and engineering goods. Moreover, China has begun to crowd out India for soft loans from the International Development Association (IDA), the World Bank affiliate. In general, Chinese membership in the multilateral lending agencies has meant that India and other developing nations must compete for increasingly limited resources.

Despite such regional dynamics, India, particularly under Rajiv Gandhi, has responded in an expansive manner. In a September 1985 interview, Gandhi said India's relations with China "have been improving steadily." The *National Herald*, which often reflects the ruling Congress party's views, said in a 1985 editorial, "The steady growth in cultural and economic contacts between India and China have opened up the possibility of the two countries forging closer relations and establishing a rapport for mutual benefit."[8]

Under General Zia-ul-Haq, Pakistan regards its "special relationship" with China as a cornerstone of its foreign policy. For Pakistan, Beijing is an important counterweight to its overpowering neighbor, India, and its ties with China were reinforced by the Soviet invasion of Afghanistan, which made Islamabad a "frontline" state vis-à-vis the expansion of Soviet influence in the region. Similarly, Bangladesh enjoys close ties to China, though they are less strategic in nature. Bangladesh's ambassador to China, Enayetullah Khan, wrote in the *China Daily* that bilateral relations have "a distinctive quality and an innate strength. . . . The whole gamut of relations has been shaped . . . by the fundamentals of sovereign equality and the requirements of a Third World partnership." Khan also spoke of "the appropriateness of Chinese technology to our concrete conditions."[9]

The smaller states of the subcontinent, such as Nepal, also view

Beijing as providing political leverage vis-à-vis India as well as economic support. A Nepalese daily commented that Sino-Nepal ties are "a model of stable friendship . . . in the best spirit of South-South cooperation."[10]

Middle East

China's policies toward the Middle East reflect an unmitigated *realpolitik* and the reality that, unlike the subcontinent, events in the Persian Gulf and the Arab-Israeli conflict lie beyond China's perimeter, and therefore, Beijing's role in the region is marginal. Beijing has officially pursued a policy parallel to the nonaligned bloc, calling for negotiations to end the Iran-Iraq war, and politically supporting the Palestinian cause and denouncing Israeli expansionism. But at the same time, China has sold arms to both Iran and Iraq, and in recent years has begun to develop covert economic and military ties with Israel. Such acts are systematically denied by Beijing and met by a curious silence by Arab and Iranian actors in the region.

The absence of any public criticism of China's self-aggrandizing behavior appears to reflect local fears of alienating Beijing and an appreciation for China's diplomatic support in international fora. In the case of Egypt, for example, China has been an important arms supplier (Zhao Ziyang's 1982 visit to Egypt resulted in a deal for China to provide 60 to 80 fighter aircraft) and economic partner since the Soviets were ejected in the 1970s. Nonetheless, generally, China is peripheral to the dynamics of the region and is viewed as a marginal political actor. China's economic and technical assistance to Middle East nations is limited, but such gestures have generated significant goodwill and paved the way for expanding economic ties.

Africa

Since the late 1950s Africa has been a centerpiece of Chinese foreign policy toward the Third World. The continent has provided a showcase for China to demonstrate many of its main foreign policy themes—anticolonialism, people's war, North-South economic injustice, and South-South cooperation. From Zhou Enlai's famous 1960 African tour to Prime Minister Zhao Ziyang's trip in late 1982 and early 1983, China has successfully used its Africa ties to establish its credentials in the nonaligned club. In the 1980s, there has been a large and steady flow of African delegations to Beijing and several senior Chinese diplomatic missions as well as many working level trips to Africa.

Aid from China

In many African countries, China is viewed as a source of inspiration as a poor largely agrarian country which, having cast off the yolk of foreign oppression, backwardness, and traditionalism, has succeeded in developing its economy and achieved genuine independence. Concretely, China was an important source of military and political support for African liberation movements beginning with the Algerian revolution in the late 1950s an early 1960s. More recently, China provided significant material support to the guerrilla movements in Mozambique and Zimbabwe that now comprise the governments of those countries. China's massive showcase project, the TanZam Railway built in the 1970s, was a dramatic example of Chinese support for Africa.

Since 1960 China has provided more than a $1 billion in aid to Africa. In the past decade or so, however, there have been two important shifts in Chinese policy toward Africa. Strategically, Chinese policy is marked by a sharp decline in anti-Sovietism which characterized Chinese diplomacy in Africa in the 1970s. Economically, China has reduced its total aid to Africa and ceased large projects such as the TanZam Railway, focusing instead on small but visible aid projects and technical assistance with almost all of the 45 African states with which it has established relations. Typically these are sports stadiums, assembly halls, rice cultivation projects, irrigation projects, light industry, and road building.

Zhao Ziyang's Tour

The 1982–1983 11-nation tour by Premier Zhao Ziyang marked an important initiative for China's Africa policy and reinforced positive African attitudes towards Beijing. Zhao enunciated four new guiding principles for Chinese cooperation with Africa: China attaches no conditions to its aid, development projects should yield practical results, projects should promote self-reliance, and cooperation contracts must be observed by both sides. A host of new aid grew out of the trip, including a $33 million loan agreement and increased military cooperation concluded with Zimbabwe. In Zaire Zhao announced that China would forgive a $100 million loan to the Mobutu regime. During the trip, China revealed that it was normalizing relations with Angola, a government it had actively opposed because of its close ties to Moscow.

African Responses

The African response to China's initiative was one of almost gushing praise. In Sudan the government-controlled *As Sahafa* commented, "China's foreign policy has won appreciation and praise from the world's people." Zaire's President Mobutu described China's cooperation as "the best in the world." Zambian President Kenneth Kaunda called China "a dependable ally," and Zimbabwean President Robert Mugabe said Beijing was "an all-weather friend."

A typical African view can be seen in a Radio Ghana commentary. It described China as an "old friend" with whom Ghana has maintained ties since 1960 and the source of two irrigation and rice projects worth some $20 million. "Ghana stands to gain immensely from cooperation with China," the commentary added. "The changes in China over the past 35 years have been profound and her successes tremendous. . . . The most striking success is that she can properly feed and clothe over 1.1 billion people."[11]

South Africa

There is, however, African concern that China still maintains a residue of anti-Sovietism and exports its own perceived fears of a Soviet threat to Africa. During the African tour of Vice Premier Tian Jiyun in December 1984 a Nigerian radio commentary, while calling for closer economic cooperation with China, attacked Beijing. "For a hitch-free Sino-Nigerian relationship, China must stop its ambivalent stand over the South African issue. China has been reluctant to aid liberation movements in Africa that are close to the Soviet Union." The broadcast added, "China must remember the proverbial saying that a drowning man can grab a snake in his bid for survival."[12]

In the case of South Africa, Beijing historically had close ties to the Pan-Africanist Congress (PAC) and provided no support for the African National Congress (ANC), the largest black African group enjoying close historic ties to Moscow and substantial backing within South Africa. In the early 1980s, China continues its close ties with the PAC, but senior Chinese officials have met with ANC leaders. During his Africa trip Zhao Ziyang met with the head of the ANC and with leaders of SWAPO, the nationalist guerrilla group in Namibia that has been strongly backed by the Soviets.

Angola

By far the most remarkable metamorphosis of Chinese policy is seen in its relations with Angola. The Popular Movement for the Liberation of Angola (MPLA) government in Angola had long established close ties with the Soviet Union and Cuba before the 1975 civil war and great power intervention. China, however, had contacts with two rival groups—UNITA and FNLA—in the pre-independence period. Despite the fact that the MPLA was clearly the only Marxist-oriented of the Angolan guerrilla groups during the initial stages of the civil war in 1974–1975, China provided military aid and training to the two groups, based on the prevailing Chinese notion that the Soviet Union was the greatest threat to the world. Beijing denounced as "mercenaries" the Cuban troops fighting on behalf of the MPLA regime, which came to power in November 1975, and downplayed the South African invasion of Angola.

The African consensus on the Angola issue was to recognize the MPLA regime as the legitimate government of Angola and admit the newly independent nation into the Organization of African Unity (OAU). China grudgingly accepted the African decision and ceased its active support for UNITA and FNLA. Gradually, Beijing began to respond to Angolan overtures and finally normalized relations with Angola, a move that was announced with some fanfare during Zhao's 1982–1983 Africa trip. Then, during Tian's mission in December 1984, China and Angola reached accord on a significant aid program. Beijing agreed to supply Angola with rice and corn seed for experimental planting, to refurbish several factories, donate two thousand tons of wheat, and to provide an $18 million interest-free loan to Angola.

In addition, the accord provided for technical and managerial training for Angola. All told, it was as substantial an amount of aid as China provides to any African country. Angolan officials heaped lavish praise on China. The Angola case reflects a new realism in Chinese Africa policy and also the current Chinese position that the Soviet Union is no greater threat to the Third World than the United States, or at least a decision not to infuse its policy with such anti-Sovietism. Moreover, China's initiative underscores its South-South emphasis in Africa.

Such moves draw deep gratitude in Africa, where drought, famine, and debt ravage the least-developed continent on earth. Africa has been largely denied commercial lending due to the gravity of its economic crisis. Thus Chinese economic aid and support for a new international economic order garners tremendous diplomatic rewards for Beijing in Africa. At the same time, China is able to reinforce its role as nonaligned partner and, via its economic aid, begin to carve out new markets for Chinese light and medium industrial goods.

Latin America

Until the 1970s, China had little contact with Latin America, and conversely, Latin American states viewed China as a distant power of little direct consequence to the region, though it welcomed Beijing's political support on regional and North-South issues in global fora. But in the post-Mao era, China has pursued a much more active policy toward Latin America as part of its general thrust to reinforce its ties to the nonaligned world. Chinese policy has been characteristically nonideological, supporting the Latin American consensus on regional issues such as the Contadora peace process for Central America and North-South economic issues and cultivating South-South cooperation. Another motivating factor in Chinese policy is Taiwan's active presence in the region—maintaining ties with 13 Latin American countries.

In recent years China has had minimal contact with leftist anti-Soviet parties in Latin America, and has ignored active revolutionary groups such as the Maoist-oriented Sendero Luminiso (Shining Path) in Peru and the Farabundo Marti Movement for National Liberation (FMLN) guerrilla front in El Salvador. Instead, China has increased exchanges with ruling parties in Latin America including pro-Soviet Nicaragua in order to improve state-to-state relations. In this effort, China is fueled by a belated recognition that many Latin American states, Chile, for example, are of economic interest to China as potential sources of strategic materials, while industrializing countries such as Brazil and Argentina are suitable economic partners.

The Latin American attitude toward China was graphically underscored at the 1981 Cancun North-South summit. Though the meeting was of paramount importance to Latin America, Latin American press coverage of China's role was remarkably scant. The geographic and cultural gaps between China and Latin America explain the lack of attention paid to Beijing, although there is a general appreciation for China's support at the United Nations and other international fora.

New Emphases

China's new emphasis on the region is underscored by consecutive trips to Latin America in 1985 by Foreign Minister Wu Xueqian, State Councillor Gu Mu, and Premier Zhao Ziyang, resulting in the signing of numerous economic and cultural cooperation agreements and expanded ties with Argentina, Brazil, Colombia, Mexico, and Venezuela. Most notable was a nuclear accord signed with Brazil (in 1984 a similar agreement had been reached with Argentina). In addition, an increasing number of Latin American delegations visited Beijing during the mid-1980s. China has established diplomatic relations with 18 Latin American and Caribbean nations and economic ties with 40 countries.

Indicative of China's initiatives in Latin America were high-level delegations from Ecuador, Mexico, and Antigua and Barbuda to Beijing in 1985. Ecuadorean Foreign Minister Edgar Teran praised increased Sino-Ecuadorean cooperation and praised China's non-aligned foreign policy, noting its support for the new international economic order. China and Ecuador signed a protocol on economic and technical cooperation and initialed a contract to purchase equipment from China for a small hydroelectric power station.

Similarly, Antigua Deputy Prime Minister Lester Bird reached agreement with China on an aid package, whereby China would provide a $2 million grant for the development of agriculture, food processing, and fisheries. In addition Beijing will provide raw materials for light manufacturing industries and launch several joint manufacturing ventures. Bird praised China for its "willingness to deal with us on a basis of equality and mutual respect." The Antiguan official added, "We were also struck by the readiness to accommodate our free enterprise system. . . . No attempt was made by the government to dictate terms."[13]

Deemphasis of Anti-Soviet Rhetoric

China's efforts to demonstrate South-South cooperation are matched by the distinct diplomatic shift downplaying the Soviet role in Latin America. This is most apparent in China's current stance toward Cuba. An article in *Shijie Zhishi* argued that "Cuba has gradually readjusted its foreign policy." It argued that Cuba has sought to improve ties to the United States and to Latin American countries, has adopted "a more flexible stand" on Central America, and praised Havana for showing "well-measured support for the democratic process" in Latin American countries.[14] Noticeably absent was any reference to Cuba doing Moscow's bidding in the Third World. The article appeared at the same time as Cuba's Vice Foreign Minister Pelegrin Torras was visiting Beijing to meet with his counterparts. An additional Chinese motive in the case of Cuba appears to be to woo Havana away from the Soviet Union.

This clear shift away from an emphasis on Soviet influence is highlighted by the Cuban case. In an interview with a Venezuelan paper during his Latin American trip, Wu Xueqian conceded that China and Cuba were improving relations. Another sign of the policy shift was evidenced in a telegram of support sent from the Federation of China Trade Unions to the Sandinista Workers Central Trade Union in May 1985. Though China had not normalized relations with Nicaragua, the telegram expressed solidarity with "Nicaraguan workers in their just struggle for national independence and against U.S. interference."

Latin American Response

Such policy initiatives have not gone unnoticed by Latin American officials. Beijing's distancing from Washington in regard to Latin America has been well received by Latin American nations. In particular, Chinese virulent criticism of U.S. intervention in Central America and support for the Contadora peace process have scored diplomatic points in the region.

Conclusion

Clearly the new contours of post-Mao Chinese foreign policy have been generally well received in the Third World. By far, China appears most successful in Africa, where its nonaligned posture has been aggressively asserted. In the regions on China's perimeter—Southeast Asia, Northeast Asia, and the Indian subcontinent—China is viewed as both an ally of the nonaligned bloc on global issues and as a regional power acting in often narrow self-interest. In regions where China's role is marginal—the Middle East and Latin America in particular—Beijing's foreign policy is accepted at face value. The shape of South-South cooperation is not yet well defined. As the patterns of such cooperation unfold, it is likely that Beijing will increasingly be viewed as a competitor as is already the case in Asia. But at the same time, to the extent that North-South economic and financial issues persist, and the rich-poor gap widens, China's support for nonaligned positions will continue to be welcomed and inject credibility into Chinese foreign policy, however self-serving it may also be.

As China modernizes, there is a growing tendency throughout the Third World to view Beijing in South-South terms as an economic competitor and ascendant great power. In North-South terms, however, China is increasingly viewed as a champion of Third World views on economic and financial issues. Moreover, the success of its economic reforms, in the face of many Third World economic failures, makes China something of a role model. This duality in Third World views of China is likely to persist in the near future.

Endnotes

1. *Merkada* (Jakarta), May 3, 1985.
2. Kuala Lumpur International Service, April 30, 1985, cited in Foreign Broadcast Information Service (hereafter cited as *FBIS*), *Daily Report: Asia and Pacific*, May 6, 1985, p. O1.
3. *Nhan Dan* (Hanoi), July 18, 1984, as cited in FBIS/*Asia and Pacific*, July 19, 1984, p. K7.
4. Senior Malaysian and Indonesian officials in interview with the author.
5. *Times Journal* (Manila), June 9, 1985.
6. *Washington Post*, April 28, 1985.
7. *Wall Street Journal*, August 8, 1985.

8. *National Herald* (New Delhi), May 14, 1985.

9. *China Daily* (Beijing), October 4, 1985.

10. *The Rising Nepal* (Katmandu), August 2, 1985.

11. Accra Domestic Service, November 8, 1984, in FBIS/*Middle East and Africa*, November 9, 1984, p. T2.

12. Quoted in *New Africa* (London), March 1985.

13. Bridgetown CANA, July 5, 1985, as cited in FBIS/*Latin America*, July 8, 1985, pp. S10–11.

14. Qi Yan, "New Trends in Cuba's Foreign Relations," *Shijie Zhishi* (Beijing), no. 9, May 1, 1985, pp. 7–8, in FBIS/*China*, May 15, 1985, p. J1.

INDEX

327.5.10172 C   116531

China and the Third World

327.510.172 C   116531

China and the Third World

DATE DUE		BORROWER'S NAME	
SEP 1 0 1984		J. Wilks 230-5272	